NELLIE CASHMAN

PROSPECTOR AND TRAILBLAZER

**Missouri Center
for the Book**

ら・ら・ら

**Missouri Authors
Collection**

NELLIE CASHMAN

PROSPECTOR AND TRAILBLAZER

by

Suzann Ledbetter

Texas
Western
Press

THE UNIVERSITY OF TEXAS AT EL PASO

SOUTHWESTERN STUDIES NO. 98

First Edition
Library of Congress Catalog Card No. 92-062201
ISBN 0-87404-194-5

 Texas Western Press books are printed on acid-free paper.

CONTENTS

ACKNOWLEDGMENTS

Without the assistance of many generous researchers and professional historians, Nellie's story could not have been told. I extend my sincerest appreciation and regards to Deborah Shelton and Barbara J. Bush of the Arizona Historical Society; Wallace Clayton, editor and publisher of the *National Tombstone Epitaph*; Angela Soto of the (Tucson) *Arizona Daily Star*; Lee Mortensen, Nevada Historical Society librarian; Brian A. Young, Reference Services supervisor, British Columbia Archives and Records Service; Dennis F. Walle, archivist and manuscripts Curator, University of Alaska at Anchorage; Joan M. Antonson, state historian at the Alaska Department of Natural Resources; Rose Shreier, Alaska Department of Education librarian; Lewis Bresee, editor of the *Wrangell Sentinel*; and the staffs of the Springfield (Mo.)-Greene County Library System reference department and Shepard History Room.

Robert Fisher, a freelance researcher for the Arizona Historical Society, was key to the accumulation of that facility's Cashman holdings and other materials vital to my research.

Without the support and encouragement of fellow writers and friends Charlie J. Farmer, Paul W. Johns, Veda Boyd Jones, Ray and Ross Rosenbaum, and members of the Tri-County Writers Feedback Group, this book would still be in the "one of these days" stage. Thankfully, peers do not accept excuses—only results.

Lastly, I am grateful to my family for allowing me to lock myself in my office in blissful, obsessive oblivion until this project was complete. Special kudos go to my husband for organizing and alphabetizing the book's bibliographic material.

To
Dale Walker
and in memory
of
Ogden Scoville
*

As pretty as a Celtic cameo, Irish-born Nellie Cashman became an American pioneer, philanthropist, entrepreneur, and gold prospector. This portrait was painted
from a photograph her Tombstone, Arizona restaurant's Chinese cook took with
him during a visit to his homeland. (Photograph courtesy of the Arizona
Historical Society.)

PREFACE

"There haven't been many like her nor will there be again," proclaimed "Frontier Angel," a tribute to Nellie Cashman published after her death by the *Arizona Star*. "She had beauty without ostentation, wisdom without education, and a flaming unquenchable spirit that was nonetheless familiar with the paths of true humility."[1]

With her black hair sculpted into a soft bun, long-lashed dark eyes, and an Irish creamy complexion, Cashman was as pretty as a Victorian cameo. And when necessary, she was tougher than two-penny nails.[2]

Whether prospecting for gold in the arid Southwest or frozen North, or managing boarding houses and restaurants from Tombstone, Arizona to Dawson, Alaska, she survived and thrived on more adventures than a dime novelist could imagine.

A Fairbanks, Alaska reporter once described her as "hard as flint, with endurance on the trail equal to that of any man, but with an inexhaustible fund of good humor and a cheery word and a helping hand for anyone in need."[3]

Cashman's spunk, stamina, and derring-do captured newspaper reporters' interest shortly after her arrival in Tombstone in 1880. The resultant accounts of her escapades and altruism made her the apple of an adoring public's eye, but a few writers thought it necessary to spice the narration with a modicum of misinformation, conjecture and plain old rhubarbery.

It is hardly libelous to note that *Tombstone Epitaph* founder John Clum's flowery editorials occasionally petalled praise upon friends and acquaintances he admired (including Nellie Cashman and the Earp brothers), while fiery lambastings scuttled those he considered scoundrels.

But regardless of anecdotal embellishments and a scattering of conflicting dates and details, Nellie Cashman's grit, entrepreneurship and philanthropy are deserving of a place in the West's biographic spotlight.

As Fred J. Dodge, an undercover agent for Wells, Fargo & Company and citizen of Tombstone in the 1880s, said, "Nellie Cashman was one of the most wonderful women I ever met. She was unique. Though she seemed to prefer to associate with men, there never was a spot on her moral character. I knew her in Nevada and in California before either of us reached Tombstone. In every place where I knew her she was the queen of the Irish miners, and held the respect of the 'Cousin Jacks' (Cornishmen) as well. Indeed, this high opinion of her was held by all right-thinking men. She was very outspoken, and sometimes made enemies by her uncensored expressions of opinion. I have always regarded Nellie as a most remarkable and admirable woman."[4]

ONE

Half A World From Home

Born in Queenstown, County Cork, Ireland, in about 1850, Nellie Cashman carried more than satchels of clothing when she emigrated to America. She held an unshakeable belief that a pot of gold awaited her at the end of the rainbow. All she must do was find it.[1]

According to Thomas J. Brennan, Jr.'s *Born Under The Bell Jar*, "Cashman" is a relatively rare Irish surname, more commonly of English, German, or Jewish derivation. Brennan estimated no more than five thousand Cashmans were born in Ireland from 1800 to 1960, and most were native to County Cork or County Kerry.[2]

The few published articles on her early life usually cite Nellie, her sister Fannie, and her mother Frances as sailing together and Boston as their port of entry, but date discrepancies have ranged from 1857 to 1869. With such a distinctive last name, verifying the trio's travels should have proven an easy task. However, microfilmed immigration records of those disembarking in Boston from 1848 to 1891 note several Cashman-surnamed passengers, but none named "Nellie," or "Frances."[3]

A "Fanny" Cashman, age twenty, did sail from Ireland on the *S.S. Favourite*, which docked in Boston on 12 May 1851. Two passengers referenced only as "Miss" Cashman arrived in America during that recording period, as did seven "Ellen" Cashmans, ranging in age from three to forty-five.[4] It is possible Nellie Cashman's given name was "Ellen" but that she preferred the former as a nickname. Years later, Fanny named one of her daughters "Ellen," and Fanny's son Michael followed suit with his eldest daughter.

1

The imprecision of such historic documentation is unfortunate but understandable, considering that during the 1850s and 1860s alone, over nine hundred thousand Irish immigrants fled what Cashman later termed Ireland's "unequal contest between want and oppression."[5]

How, when, and with whom Cashman traveled during her journey from the Emerald Isle remains a mystery, but she was residing in Boston by the early 1860s.

When Civil War enlistment decreased available manpower, women were hired to fill what were considered traditionally male occupations. Frank Cullen Brophy's article, "God And Nellie," records an anecdote Cashman told him of her first job in America:[6]

I remember when I met General Ulysses S. Grant. I was a bellhop in Boston at the time. He was easy to talk to, like everyone I ever knew, and when I told him I wanted to do things, because I had to if I wanted to live, he said, "Why don't you go West, young woman? The West needs people like you."

Well, we had gone west when we left Ireland, and I certainly didn't expect to spend the rest of my life being a bellhop or an Irish servant girl in Boston.[7]

Promontory Point's golden spike had hardly pinioned the transcontinental rails when Nellie and Fanny Cashman acted on General Grant's advice.[8]

In 1869 the Union Pacific's first class and coach fares, just from Omaha, Nebraska, to the coast, were priced at $100 and $75 respectively, too princely a sum for working girls' pocketbooks. However, a special immigrant rate of $40 entitled bearers to space in a springless railroad car fitted with backless board seats.[9]

The only way these passengers could sleep was by lying in the cramped floor space between benches, with their feet sprawling into the aisle. Because there was no dining car, railside shacks (ambitiously dubbed "eating stations") were, in the words of one traveler, "Miserable shanties with tables dirty, waiters not only dirty, but saucy. The tea tasted as though it were made from the leaves of sage brush — literally, sage tea. The biscuit was made without soda, but with plenty of alkali, harmonizing with the great quantity of alkali dust we had already swallowed."[10]

To partake of such indigestible victuals, Nellie and Fanny each had to part with a dollar of their hard-earned wages, then gobble their food before the impatient conductor hollered, "All aboard!"[11]

In fact, passengers could not depend on an announcement preceding the train's departure. As Robert Louis Stevenson noted in *The Amateur Emigrant*, ". . . the train stole from the station without note of warning and you had to keep an eye upon it even while you ate. The annoyance is considerable; and the disrespect both wanton and petty."[12]

Immigrant trains were also routinely shunted onto sidings to allow express (or higher ticket-priced) trains the right-of-way, which added days to the trip's duration. After chugging over two thousand miles, at an average speed of eighteen to twenty-two miles per hour, sighting the "City by the Bay" was undoubtedly a blessed event for every exhausted, backsore bench rider.

In those days, San Francisco was undergoing the slow transformation from rough-and-tumble mining boomtown to bustle-tamed, civilized metropolis — albeit still a predominantly male-populated one.[13]

This gender disparity worked in Fanny Cashman's favor. In 1870, scant months after she and Nellie arrived, Fanny married Thomas Cunningham, a fellow Irish immigrant, and settled there to raise a family.[14]

Nellie's beauty and unbanded ring finger must have attracted a fair share of suitors as well, but she hadn't left her beloved Ireland and traveled halfway around the world just to snare a husband and keep house. As she later informed an *Arizona Star* reporter, she "preferred being pals with men to being cook for one man."[15]

She was barely five feet tall and weighed less than a hundred pounds but Cashman set sizeable goals for herself: to make lots of money, and to help anyone who needed it.

Pursuant to the first, Cashman's skill with a spatula got her hired as a cook in several Nevada mining camps including Virginia City, Comstock, and Pioche. Since the shortage of women providing miners various "creature comforts" inflated the cost of those services accordingly, it it is reasonable to assume she earned a fair income.

Cashman also prospected in the rugged, scrubby hills surrounding Pioche, but was shrewd enough to realize that a miner's income was as fickle as a doxy's affections.

Embracing the cautious speculator's motto, "Never risk more than you can afford to lose and always have a trade to fall back on," wherever her search for gold led her, she established a boardinghouse, a restaurant, or both.

The 4 September 1872 classified section of Pioche, Nevada's *Ely Record* included an advertisement reading:

Miner's Boarding House

Panaca Flat

Having fitted in good style this old established boarding house, the undersigned would be pleased to meet her friends.

Board By The Day Or Week[16]

The announcement must have referred to one of Cashman's enterprises, as her presence in the area at the time is documented. Yet, "the undersigned" below the copy is stated as "Fanny Cashman," and Fanny Cashman Cunningham was by now two years wed, a resident of San Francisco, and mother of her first son, Tom, born the same year.[17]

Why Fanny was listed as the owner of Miner's Boarding House is a mystery, especially when Nellie's culinary abilities were so highly regarded she had earned the nickname "Nellie Pioche."

In his article, "Frontier Angel," Frank Cullen Brophy recollected Cashman's telling him, "Those miners were a rough lot, but they were good men. I liked them and they liked me, and if the silver veins had not begun to pinch out, I might have been there 'til I died. But, that's the way it is in mining — just when you don't expect it, you strike it rich, and then when you think you are about to become a silver queen or a copper queen, the vein peters out and you hear there's a big new strike in Alaska or some other Godforsaken place."[18]

One tale of Cashman's trading her frying pan for a gold pan may be of the "tall" variety. Or, considering her sense of humor and hunger for adventure, it may be more factual than fanciful.

As friend Fred Lockley told a (Victoria, B.C.) *Daily Colonist* reporter, Cashman and a half-dozen equally wanderlustful male friends decided to leave Nevada and seek their gold prospecting fortunes elsewhere. Except the group couldn't agree which was riper for plundering: the reputedly rich veins in South Africa or British Columbia's gold-laden Cassiar District.[19]

Supposedly, the tails-up landing of a twenty-dollar gold piece settled the dispute: Six men and Miss Cashman set off for Canada.[20]

More likely, reports of gold strikes in those northern regions spiked Cashman's now incurable gold fever. She also must have heard, and dismissed, warnings of that locale's bone-numbing cold and the Stikeen Trail's treachery — a passage so formidable, that after hearing a source's description of the route, a Skagway newspaperman wrote, "His account of the Stikeen trail would bring tears to the eyes of potatoes."[21]

As time went on, Cashman proved that nothing nature devised could faze her. Upon meeting her, a *Daily Colonist* reporter marveled, "The woman was on snowshoes and as jolly as a sand-buoy. At the Boundary Pass she lost the trail and was twenty-eight hours exposed to the pitiless pelting of a storm, without shelter or blankets."[22]

She was equally as hale and hearty in 1877 when, dressed in a mackinaw, men's trousers, boots, and a fur hat, she was the first white woman to behold the blinding white majesty of the snow-covered Cassiar wilderness.[23]

Cashman detailed that expedition in a later newspaper interview:

> I went north to Cassiar with a party of 200 miners from Nevada. We penetrated a practically unknown country. When the party settled down in what was then a very rich region, I alternately mined and kept a boarding house for miners.
>
> In the fall of the year I came out to civilization, that is to Victoria, but learning that a large number of our party was sick with the scurvy, I hastened back after securing six men to accompany me.[24]
>
> It took 77 days to reach camp as the winter was very severe. At [Fort] Wrangel the United States custom officers tried to dissuade me from taking what they termed "my mad trip" and, in fact, when we had been several days up the river on our journey they sent up a number of men to induce me to turn back.[25]

(Note: Actually, an Indian had reported a white woman's death to Fort Wrangel's commander. The officer knew Nellie was the only white woman within hundreds of miles and immediately sent soldiers to find her body. Find her they did — relaxing beside a roaring campfire, contentedly sipping a cup of tea.)[26]

> We pushed on in the coldest kind of weather with hardly any trail to follow and after sleeping 66 days in the snow, reached the camp in time to be of service to the men, some of whom where half-dead for want of proper supplies.[27]
>
> They are talking a great deal about sleeping bags, etc., for that northern country, but all I used on that terrible trip was a pair of blankets. Some days we travelled only five miles, for we took with us about 1,500 pounds of supplies.[28]

That Cashman's rescue party accomplished its mission of mercy was no less than miraculous. The weather was especially severe that winter, necessitating the breaking of a trail through the snow accumulation along the frozen Stikeen River.

With snowshoes lashed to her boots and dragging a heavy sled by a harness slung around her neck, Cashman obviously did not ask for or expect that any quarter be given the only female member of the team.

As she told Fred Lockley several years later, "One night the men put my tent on the side of a steep hill where snow was ten feet deep. The next morning one of the men came to where my tent was to bring me coffee.[29]

"It had snowed heavily in the night and, to his surprise, he couldn't find the tent. Finally, they discovered me a quarter of a mile down the hill, where my tent, my bed and myself and all the rest of my belongings had been carried by a snowslide. No, they didn't dig me out; by the time they got there I had dug myself out."[30]

Victoria's *Daily Colonist* shed more light on Cashman's purposeful objective: "Her extraordinary freak of attempting to reach the diggings in midwinter and in the face of dangers and obstacles . . . is attributed by her friends as insanity."[31]

When the stricken miners' camp was reached, she cooked, served, and in some cases, spoonfed them the vitamin C-enriched foodstuffs critical to their recovery.[32]

In particular, the potatoes she had brought were so prized as both scurvy preventative and antidote that one miner considered them as "precious as grain in the sacks of Israel's sons in Egypt."[33]

Cashman was quite proud the camp's death toll dropped to zero after her party's arrival. Grateful-to-be-alive prospectors told anyone who would listen of her defiance of the elements and a government official's orders, and of her tireless and compassionate care.

As a result, the sobriquet, "Angel of the Cassiar" reverently followed mentions of her name. Many years later, a Cassiar survivor said on his death bed, "If Nellie Cashman were only here, I'd get well."[34]

Portrayed by writer Edward Morgan as a "lone figure in the wilderness, who had surmounted all the obstacles with which nature had beset her path, and had talked out of existence all those put in her way by men," Cashman made her femininity evident regardless of how many layers of bulky outwear she wore.[35]

In her article, "The Amazing Adventures of a Good Woman," Harriet Rochlin stated, "Her hardy laugh, Irish brogue, and her ability to express herself in forceful oral and written language were also often noted. Rarely, however, without adding a reassuring comment about her essential femininity."[36]

However, Victorian conventions regarding ladylike demeanor were as inflexible as whaleboned corsets and a virtuous, enterprising pioneer like Nellie Cashman presented an anomaly, an exception to the "rules."

After all, in that era unmarried women who routinely cohabitated with men were known variously as "soiled doves," "Jezebels," or "strumpets." Ironically, according to an anecdote in Frances H. Backhouse's article, "Women of the Klondike," Cashman was once turned away from a trail camp after supper because the men "feared for her reputation — or theirs — if she was allowed to remain in camp after dark."[37]

Her atypical lifestyle and prospecting pursuits made her a trailblazer in every sense of the word, but not a whisper of scandal ever tarnished Cashman's name or sterling reputation.

"She went alone where only bad women went alone, and did what good women do alone," said biographer Harriet Rochlin.[38]

After decades of predominately male companionship, when bluntly asked if she had ever "feared for her virtue," she answered, "Bless your soul, no! I never had a word said to me that was out of the way. The 'boys' would see to it that anyone who ever offered to insult me could never be able to repeat the offense.[39]

"The farther you go away from civilization, the bigger-hearted and more courteous you find the men. Every man I met up north was my protector and any man I ever met, if he needed my help, got it, whether it was a hot meal, nursing, mothering, or whatever else he needed. After all, we pass this way only once, and it's up to us to help our fellows when they need our help."[40]

TWO

The Belle Of The Town

Nellie Cashman reentered the States a wealthier woman for having gained the admiration and respect of her peers and extensive hands-on, mining experience.

What assayable assets she had prized from the ground, along with contributions solicited from other Cassiar prospectors, were donated to Victoria's Sisters of St. Ann for their St. Joseph's Hospital building fund.[1]

With the boom all but busted in Nevada, Cashman took a stagecoach south to investigate rumors of strikes in California's arid hinterlands.

As she later told Bernice Cosulich, a reporter for the *Arizona Star*, she and the other passengers were jostling along a rough-cut track across the barrens when the driver suddenly reined his team to a halt. "'What dump is this?' I called, 'The City of Angels?' There was nothing, absolutely nothing, but dogs in sight. It was the first time I knew that dogs had souls.[2]

"I came very near being a pioneer of California, but those dogs and Los Angeles cured me. So we bumped along over trails into Yuma. Such a place — mosquitoes by the billions everywhere. When we sat down to supper, I asked the driver if he hadn't seasoned the beans rather heavily with pepper.

"He looked up and laughed, 'Mosquitoes it is, my friend,' he said. But we ate the beans just the same. Had to. There was nothing else cooked."[3]

In a valley bordered by four mountain ranges, sleepy Tucson was still very much a Mexican pueblo, but news of forthcoming

9

Southern Pacific Railroad service translated as greater profit potential to an energetic entrepreneur like Nellie Cashman.

On 29 July 1879, *The Daily Arizona Citizen* announced the opening of the first business in town owned by a white woman:

DELMONICO RESTAURANT

Miss Nellie Cashman

Has just opened a new Restaurant on the South side of
Church Plaza

TUCSON————————-ARIZONA

Miss Cashman will personally superintend the Cooking
and Dining Departments.

Patronage Solicited.[4]

Two bits bought "a chuck that would stick to a man's ribs," but prospectors with bellies as empty as their pockets dined "on the house" at Delmonico's.[5]

The restaurant was a success despite Cashman's soft-heartedness, but Tucson's molasses-in-January pace was too short on excitement for her tastes. Within months, she relocated to eighty miles-distant Tombstone.

A fond farewell was bidden her by Tucson's *Arizona Star*: "Mrs. M. J. Smith has purchased the Delmonico restaurant from Miss Nellie Cashman. The latter lady goes to Tombstone, where she has established a business. While Miss Nellie Cashman's many friends will regret her leaving the city, Tombstone will have cause to rejoice, as she makes a business stir wherever she goes."[6]

Tombstone was born of prospector Ed Schieffelin's conviction that the hills surrounding the San Pedro Valley were heavily veined with silver. Unfortunately, they were also rife with marauding Apaches who had no intention of sharing territory they considered exclusively their own.

Schieffelin was told, "All you'll ever find in them hills'll be your tombstone. Geronimo'll git you ef you don't watch out, and leave your bones for the buzzards to pick."[7]

Tombstone, Arizona's "Million Dollar Stope" which tunnelled beneath busy Toughnut Street. Stope mining was done in timber-supported passages which honeycombed for miles under the surrounding counryside, interconnecting with other mines. (Photograph courtesy of the Library of Congress.)

If only that skeptic had been present four months later when Schieffelin examined a rock fragment cobwebbed by veins of rich, horn silver! Ore samples from the mine he claimed and christened 'The Lucky Cuss' assayed $15,000 to the ton, a bonanza beyond even his wildest dreams.[8]

In April 1879, with news of Schieffelin's discovery came wagonloads of tradesmen, craftsmen, service-providers, and hardy Cornish Jacks seeking an honest dollar. In their wake drifted the camp followers: dance hall doxies, thieves, slick-fingered gamblers, pimps, claim jumpers, and shootists.

Because lumber was dear, wood-framed, canvas-walled structures rose literally overnight from the powdery dust. As the first issue of the *Weekly Nugget* boasted, "Thirty four buildings are now under contract, and will be in process as soon as the lumber arrives, of which there is great scarcity at the present time. We live mostly in canvas houses up here, and when lunatics like those who fired so promiscuously the other night are on the rampage, it ain't safe anyhow!'"⁹

While a frantic race to shelter the flood of newcomers commenced above ground, below it, miners were cutting mazes of tunnels beneath streets and stores. Tough Nut Street, named for another Schieffelin claim, was bordered by a gaping stope from which tons of silver were extracted.¹⁰

Heavy ore wagons pulled by sixteen- and twenty-mule teams rumbled constantly along Allen Street, Tombstone's wide main thoroughfare. Their passage was like a drumrolling accompaniment to the plinkety piano music, raucous laughter, and occasional gunshots echoing from the north side's never-closed saloons, gambling houses, and theaters.

According to Odie B. Faulk's *Tombstone: Myth And Reality*, ". . . at night, he who slept too close to downtown would be awakened suddenly by some unearthly noise, musical or otherwise; by the shout of 'Promenade to the Bar' at some dance hall; by the bellowing yell of 'Keno' from the throat of a rejoicing gambler; by a pistol shot fired by some 'shoot-em-up-Dick' who had read too many dime novels and wanted to hurrah the town. It was like living in a boiler factory — the noise was harmless unless it bothered you, and then it drove you crazy."¹¹

On the south side of Allen, Tombstonians peaceably patronized the string of stores, specialty shops, and restaurants as if the Crystal Palace, the Oriental, and later, the Bird Cage Opera House could not be seen, nor their drunk and disorderly customers heard.¹²

John Clum, the founder, editor, and publisher of the newly established *Tombstone Daily* and *Weekly Epitaph* maintained that most of the residents were "perfectly good citizens; lawyers, doctors, mine workers — butchers, bakers and candlestick makers . . . and a couple of editors."¹³

In June 1880 Artemus E. Fay, editor of the rival *Daily* and *Weekly Nugget*, printed a directory of the 129 businesses and pro-

Boomtown Tombstone's Allen Street during the early 1880s. Note the signboard on the right advertising Nellie Cashman's Nevada Boot & Shoe Store. (Photograph courtesy of the Arizona Historical Society.)

fessional services (noticeably excepting the upstart *Epitaph*) already established in the year-old city.[14]

The Nevada Boot & Shoe Store, located on Allen Street above Fifth Street and owned by "Miss Nelly [*sic*] Cashman," was described as a: "Dealer in boots, shoes, hosiery and ladies' wear. A specialty of gentlemen's furnishing goods. She has a neat store, well fitted with a select assortment of goods, which she opened April 15, 1880, and is building up a good trade."[15]

Her mercantile had stiff competition. Additionally advertised in the directory were Henry L. Gehman's shoe store on Allen, between Fifth and Sixth, Charles A. Rolig's shoe store on Allen above Fifth, and John Zappeinen, a boot and shoe maker, also on Allen between Fifth and Sixth streets.[16]

This retail redundancy may have caused Cashman's divestiture of the store and the establishment of the Arcade, a restaurant specializing in steaks and chops. Shortly after its debut, however, Cashman sold The Arcade — as it happened, a most fortuitous occurrence. Within a few weeks, the cigar-puffing bartender was hefting a barrel of bad whiskey onto the porch when embers from his stogie fell inside.[17] The alcohol exploded, setting off a fiery chain reaction which left the Arcade, and much of Tombstone's business district, a smoldering ruin. While abundantly supplied with one natural resource, silver ore, the town woefully lacked a municipal water supply.[18]

Recounted Frank Waters in his book, *The Earp Brothers of Tombstone*, a newcomer once exclaimed, "'All Tombstone needs to become the garden spot of the world is good people and water.'

"'Well, stranger,' an old prospector replied, 'I reckon that's all *hell* needs.'"[19]

Cashman obviously thought Tombstone also needed another restaurant, so in partnership with cattle rancher Joseph Pascholy, she established the Russ House at the corner of Fifth and Tough Nut streets.

In a community where miners addled by whiskey stole rat-killing cats to ensure an undisturbed night's sleep, her declaration that "There are no cockroaches in my kitchen and the flour is clean," was especially meaningful. Such scrupulous sanitation, coupled with a menu featuring "the best food this side of the Pecos," allowed her to charge double the going rate of twenty-five cents per meal.[20]

The repast a paltry four bits afforded Russ House patrons is evidenced by this bill of fare, dated Sunday, 8 November 1881:

SOUPS
Chicken and Consomme
FISH
Brook Trout, Fois a l'huile
BOILED
Lamb, caper sauce
Beef a l'Espanol
Corned Beef
ENTREES
Breast of lamb, breaded a la Mayonnaise
Croquettes, Rice, Kirshwasser Sauce
Chicken Fricasse a la Creme
Salim of Chicken giblets
Calf Head in Tortue
ROASTS
Prime of Beef
Ribs of Beef
Leg of Mutton
Stuffed Lamb
Dressed Veal
Pork with Applesauce
Chicken
VEGETABLES
Sugar Peas, Tomatoes, Corn,
Turnips and Mashed Potatoes
PASTRY
Assorted Pies and Jelly Roll
PUDDING
New York Plum, Hard Sauce
Lemon Flavor

DESSERT
Grapes and Walnuts
SALADS
Lobster, Tomatoes, Beets,
and Horseradish
RELISHES
Assorted[21]

It is not surprising that more than four hundred people elbowed into the Russ House's dining room on opening day. Cashman's policy of treating down-on-their-luck prospectors as her guests assumes that number included a few of the gratis variety, as well.

The Russ House's table d'hote attests to the cosmopolitan air that Tombstone's continual influx of new residents and two million dollars in mine revenues were starting to effect.

The latest fashions from San Francisco were stocked by shops along Allen Street and worn to dances held at the Cosmopolitan, Grand, and Occidental hotels.

Delicacies such as capers, oysters, and French wines and liqueurs could be found on mercantile shelves alongside the more pedestrian sugar, salt and cornstarch.

Despite their ramshackle beginnings, the "better" saloons and gambling halls now boasted long bars of polished mahogany, imported carpets, liquor of the highest quality, and crystal glassware in which to serve it.[22]

Organizations including the Masons, Knights of Columbus, Knights of Pythias, Daughters of Rebekah, and Independent Order of Odd Fellows had chapters in Tombstone, and churches of the Methodist, Presbyterian, and Episcopalian faiths flourished.

Interestingly, church members joined with fraternal organization members in forming their own cemetery. All concerned had decided they did not want themselves or their loved ones buried in the only graveyard in town, known as Boot Hill, where none interred to date had "died of natural causes."[23]

A devout Catholic, Cashman was determined that a church of her denomination be built in Tombstone. The bishop in charge of

Tombstone's infamous Bird Cage Theatre, inspiration for the song, "She Was Only A Bird In A Gilded Cage," and the scene of riotous entertainment during the silver mining boom days. (Photograph courtesy of the Library of Congress.)

the diocese agreed a place of worship was needed and made a bargain with her: if she would get a church, he would come up with a priest.[24]

Cashman was assigned the more difficult task and had no qualms about canvassing the entire town for contributions, including the "wrong" side of Allen Street and the red-light district.[25] She was in complete agreement with the Reverend Endicott Peabody's philosophy, "The Lord's pot must be kept boiling even if it takes the Devil's kindling wood." Years later, Cashman maintained, regardless of the cause undertaken, her greatest help came "from the back street which had no name on the map."[26]

After raising seven hundred dollars by personal subscription, Cashman organized fundraisers including Tombstone's first amateur theater production (a musical comedy entitled The Irish Diamond), and a grand ball.

When all the building campaign's proceeds were tallied, ground was broken for the Sacred Heart Catholic Church at Safford and Sixth streets, and the bishop assigned Father Gallagher to the newly created post.

Grateful that her faith was represented among the town's houses of worship, Cashman made fast friends with the priest and ignored his occasional "falls from grace."

John Pleasant Gray, one-time Tombstone postmaster, remembered seeing her "go by in the evening helping Father Gallagher home . . . for good old Father Gallagher at times would take a drop too much."[27]

A veritable one-woman chamber of commerce, Salvation Army, and Red Cross combined, Cashman continually solicited contributions for a variety of good works.

True to one connotation of her surname, she served as treasurer for both the Red Path Branch Irish National Land League (a miner's aid organization) and the Miner's Hospital Association.[28] Regarding the former, Cashman not only kept a reckoning of the accounts, but she likely "passed the hat" with regularity as attested to by this *Tombstone Nugget* mention: "Miss Nellie Cashman, treasurer for the Wolf Tone Branch of the Irish Land League has forwarded to executive authorities of the League a sum of two hundred dollars. Pretty good for a small band of Irish-Americans."[29]

Evidence of her arm-twisting tactics appeared four paragraphs below in a piece slugged "Wake Up":

> Miss Nellie Cashman, treasurer of the Land League at this place, says Tucson is the only town in Arizona that has not contributed funds in aid of the good cause. She further avers that there are over a thousand Irish-Americans in that city and trusts that the *Citizen* [Tucson's newspaper] will wake them up to a full realization of their duty.[30]

Whatever the need or nationality, the sick, the hungry, and the destitute were assured comfort under her wing. A case in point is her collection of five hundred dollars to defray medical expenses and feed the family of a miner who fell down a shaft and broke both legs.[31]

"If she asked for a contribution — we contributed," said John Clum. "If she had tickets to sell — we bought tickets. If she needed actors for a play — we volunteered to act. And although Nellie's pleas were frequent, none ever refused her."[32]

Between her civic activities and the management of a bustling business, she had little time for prospecting. Rather than wielding a pick and shovel herself, she regularly grubstaked expeditions and in turn, expected a percentage of the profits if pay dirt was struck.

Decades later, when asked if those men, some of whom became millionaires, would remember their first benefactor, she laughed and said, "Why should they? It was a square deal. I furnished the food, they did the work, and we shared half up to each. Nothing to feel grateful to me for."[33]

In his book, *Billy King's Tombstone*, C.L. Sonnichsen said, "The wildest bunch of desperadoes ever concentrated in a similar space flourished in Cochise County in the Eighties."[34]

While this may have been true, throughout her residency there, anecdotes regarding Cashman's popularity with Tombstone's citizens, both the forgotten and the infamous, have been circulated repeatedly.

For example, on one occasion, a drummer allegedly disparaged the quality of his Russ House meal. A lanky, mustachioed man seated at a nearby table took umbrage at the salesman's remarks, drew his revolver, and pointed it in such a way as to cause the complainant an immediate loss of appetite.

"What did you say about Miss Nellie's food, mister?" the gun-wielder asked.

"Food's delicious," the man replied. "Good as I've ever tasted."

A satisfied smirk spread across Doc Holliday's face as he eased his weapon back into its holster and drawled, "Yep, that's what I thought you said."[35]

Cashman may not have encouraged such shenanigans be performed in her defense, but it is likely she secretly delighted in them. As for her shootist friends, in his article, "God And Nellie" writer Frank Cullen Brophy recalled Cashman's telling him, "I get a big laugh these days with all this nonsense and horseplay about Wyatt Earp and Doc Holliday and poor John Ringo and the others. They weren't bad fellows, but most of them had to fight it out to keep ahead of the game."[36]

Unquestionably the belle of the town, enmeshing herself in its social, commercial and charitable activities, Cashman kept whirling happily in the middle of the action.

Then, in late 1880, a telegram arrived which turned her independent, well-ordered world upside down.[37]

THREE

"I'm Still Here
To Tell The Story . . ."

Thomas Cunningham was dead. The "poor man's disease," tuberculosis, had claimed another victim. Grief-stricken and tubercular herself, Fanny was cast into the role of singly parenting five children and she possessed neither the funds nor the skills to support them.

Without hesitation, her sister Nellie sold the Russ House and rushed to San Francisco.

In the decade since Cashman's short residency there, that city's financial and commercial districts had spread geographically outward and upward, with multi-storied buildings stair-stepping the skyline, lending occupants a bird's-eye view of the bay.[1]

Yet, for all its capital and civic improvements, San Francisco's economy rose and fell as precipitously as its cobblestoned avenues. Langley's *City Directory* for 1878-79 stated, ". . . marked with an extraordinary depression in almost all branches of labor, the city was thronged with a multitude of men out of employ such as had never before been known. . . ."[2]

Realizing immediately that her prospects as breadwinner for the Cunningham brood were brighter in Tombstone, Cashman straw-bossed the packing and shipment of the fatherless family's household goods, then escorted them to Arizona Territory.

With Fanny and her children settled comfortably in a relatively austere adobe cottage behind the Russ House,[3] Cashman's responsibilities had sextupled and her enterprising efforts increased proportionately.

Constructed of adobe with a gated courtyard, Miss Cashman's home in Tombstone was modest for a family of seven. (Photograph courtesy of the Arizona Historical Society.)

Having already reacquired the Russ House (a property she bought and sold several times), she was also caretaking a frail Fanny, helping with the children, and continued offering a hand or a handout to anyone who needed it.

"Cleaning and caring for the rooms was all I could do," Cashman remarked in a later interview, "though I did find time now and then to see a pretty piece of shooting. There weren't many days that passed without bitter fights and telling shots. . . ."[4]

When Fanny's health improved, the sisters remodeled and redecorated the Russ's boardinghouse, reopening it as the American Hotel.

Less than a month later, fire broke out in a water closet of the Tivoli Saloon and just like blazes before it, swept rapidly through the business district.

The sisters and a few friends formed a bucket brigade to keep the tinder-dry boardinghouse wet. Three times the building caught fire, and three times its owners and volunteers rushed to douse the flames. [5]

Again, much of Tombstone was left in ashes. The American Hotel remained standing, but its first and second story rear rooms, and much of Nellie and Fanny's personal possessions, were virtually destroyed.[6]

Structural damages were estimated at fifteen hundred dollars, but Cashman didn't waste a second worrying about money needed to repair the hotel. Knowing too well how quickly infernos had ravaged other frontier towns, she had insured the American for *twice* that amount.[7]

It is a different kind of 'fire,' however, for which Tombstone will forever be remembered.

Versions of the shootout at the O.K. Corral probably equal the number of years since its occurrence. The date (26 October 1881), the shootists (Virgil, Wyatt, and Morgan Earp, John "Doc" Holliday, and Ike Clanton), and the trio "hurled into eternity" as a result (Frank and Tom McLowery and Billy Clanton), seem the only particulars of this corpse and cartridge occasion left unshaded by hindsight and Hollywood.[8]

Cashman's seven-year-old nephew, Mike Cunningham, didn't see the bullets fly or find their marks, but was on his way home from school when the bodies were being lifted aboard flatbed wagons. For the rest of his life he vividly remembered bringing water to the dying and wounded.[9]

From that infamous day forward, the general public, and President Chester A. Arthur branded Tombstone "a terrible place which had at least one murder a day, supported a population composed of painted women, drunks, gamblers, Chinamen, and prospectors, and held a set of customs which flew in the face of God and flouted the Constitution."[10]

While "outlanders" continued in their disparagements of the town, its ten thousand residents, including Nellie Cashman, carried on with the business of living, and the business of business as usual.

The threat of Indian raids and reprisals had not diminished as Tombstone flourished and was infinitely more worrisome than pistol-packing desperadoes. Venturing alone too far beyond the city proper, especially during the day, risked an Apache-style retribution.[11]

According to an account in the 11 January 1925 edition of the *Arizona Star*, Cashman was en route to pick up a woman friend in neighboring Fairbank and the driver was letting the horses jog along in the darkness, when suddenly "like the opening of an inferno came the cries as of those tortured in death. The driver wanted to race the team, but his passenger made him stop. As the terrifying yells of the Indian raiders grew closer and closer, the animals stamped and roared. It was Geronimo and his warriors out on a midnight raid on a farmhouse. They swept by the buggy and its two frightened persons without even seeing them. Miss Cashman said it was a close 'squeak' but declared in her fatalistic way, that if it had been meant that he should add their scalps to his belt, it would have happened.

"'I was never afraid of anything,' she declared. 'There was no need to be. I'm still here to tell the story, and I have too much to do to be afraid.'"[12]

Nevertheless, the close call may have reminded her of her own adage, "You never quite know what's going to happen next, or when your time will come to cash in your checks. It all adds interest and variety to life."[13]

Or, as various periodicals have since reported, her adventuresome spirit may have been kindled when a Mexican miner pushed some gold nuggets toward her in payment for his meal. Using a garbled rendition of Spanish and pidgin English (his dying words, according to one version), the man tried to tell Cashman whence his find came. All she could comprehend were phrases referencing a dry streambed near Santa Rosalia, in the Baja California area.[14]

Whatever the impetus, Cashman, M.E. Joyce (owner of the opulent Oriental Saloon), flamboyant attorney Marcus A. Smith (later to become Arizona's first senator), and other townsmen soon departed Tombstone on the Modoc stage for Guaymas, Mexico. There they chartered a boat to ferry them across the Gulf of California and bought burros in Santa Rosalia for the desert leg of their journey. [15]

Accounts of their adventure, or more precisely the lack thereof, have given rise to the speculations, contradictions, and campfire-told stories of "The Lost Cashman Mine," still in circulation over a century later.[16]

The gold hunters undertook the expedition during the summer months in one of the most desolate, godforsaken regions in all of North America. Their destination, the Golo Valley, was twenty-seven miles inland from Santa Rosalia.

Although advised to hire a guide, when the party learned a trail existed, they dismissed the suggestion, promising to drop markers along the way. They set off on foot, their burros laden with water and several days' supplies.[17]

The trail they followed was clear and straight for miles, then forked sharply. After some debate, they picked a track and struck off confidently. Hours passed before it dead-ended at an abandoned settlement. Before they could retrace their steps, darkness forced them to make camp.[18]

The next morning, again following the original trail, they came to a junction branched into three alternative directions. The path they chose eventually divided and in time, forked again. There were no landmarks, no indications of what direction they were heading — including whether or not it was the "right" one.

On the third day, they began rationing water.

The fourth heralded the beginnings of heat exhaustion, dehydration, and the men's decision to turn back. Except, fearing they would be followed to the Golo Valley cache, the prospectors had *not* waymarked their circuitous route.[19] Because of their greed, the party was adrift in a vast sea of sand. The men were weakening, dazed from the heat and lack of water, their dreams of glittering booty forgotten.

"Don't worry, boys," Cashman is credited with assuring them. "Right now I'm stronger than any one of you, and I can travel. A good angel will lead me to water."[20]

She was gone a full day and returned with some Mexicans leading burros bearing goatskins full of water from a mission tucked away in a nearby valley.

Or, as another version tells it, while scooping a trench in a shallow streambed to fill her canteen, Cashman spied a smattering of gold nuggets among the pebbles. She was excitedly scrabbling for more when a shadow loomed from behind her.[21]

It was a priest, Father Pedro, and he invited her to accompany him to his mission. Following a sumptuous meal, Father Pedro explained that the gold she found was the sole means of support for his parish. If its location was disclosed, the resulting stampede of prospectors would strip the natives of their only livelihood.[22]

Come sunrise, the priest presented his guest with supplies, mules, and a guide to lead her to her friends, and on to Santa Rosalia. Before she left the mission, Cashman promised Father Pedro his secret was safe with her. [23]

The fortune seekers had hardly recovered from their desert misadventure when their lives were threatened again while recrossing the Bay of California.

As John Clum relates in his tribute, ". . . they had not proceeded far on their voyage when the captain of the craft appeared in a half-crazed condition due to an over-indulgence in 'hard likker.'"[24]

The prospectors hog-tied the inebriated captain, stowed him securely below decks, and with the aid of a pair of sea-worthy sailors, navigated the boat to Guaymas.

Upon docking, the entire Tombstone party was immediately arrested and imprisoned for committing mutiny. After spending several days in a filthy, foul-smelling Mexican jail, their release was successfully negotiated by the American consul to Mexico.[25]

Ironically, a *Phoenix Herald* article published at the beginning of the expedition had cautioned, "It would be advisable for people going to the mines to post themselves as to the laws regarding placer mining in Mexico. Many people will undoubtedly go there under the impression that the laws are the same as those in the United States, but there are certain laws for locating claims in Mexico which are quite different. The gaining of the knowledge may save much trouble."[26]

Suffice it to say, an advisory to review Mexico's maritime laws would also have been timely.

Double death defiance and incarceration notwithstanding, the tatterdemalion group received its share of rib-poking and ridicule upon their empty-pocketed return to Tombstone. In fact, page two of the 14 June 1883 *Phoenix Weekly Herald* had carried this cryptic announcement datelined a day earlier from Tombstone: "The Joyce-Cashman party have returned to Guaymays [*sic*] from the Lower California gold fields and report nothing to it."[27]

Whether the padre's stash was a figment of Cashman's or her partners' sun-stroked imaginations will probably never be known, but for all the adventures she told and retold during numerous interviews over the next sixty years, regardless of their rags or riches endings, rarely did she even mention the Guaymas expedition.

Had she perished at the hands of the Apache chieftain the U.S. Army dubbed "Geronimo" (Goyathlay; One-Who-Yawns) or (as reported erroneously in newspapers all over the West) in the Baja California desert, the fate and futures of her five nieces and nephews would have been altered dramatically.

The tuberculosis Fanny valiantly fought, just as her husband had three years earlier, finally ended her life as well. It was now up to Aunt Nell to provide the five Cunningham children, ranging in age from four to twelve, with emotional, spiritual, and financial support.

However, it was Cashman's intervention affecting a quite different quintet that garnered more of the townsfolk's attention.

In the nearby town of Bisbee, on the evening of 8 December 1883, Daniel Dowd and Omer W. (Red) Sample stood in front of Goldwater & Castenada's store and pulled their six-shooters from their holsters.[28] Without warning, one of them started firing up the street and the other, down. With a hail of bullets and screaming pedestrians creating the planned diversion, James (Tex) Howard, William Delaney, and Daniel Kelly rifled the mercantile's cash drawer and safe, and looted showcases of their watches and jewelry.[29]

Leaving one woman and two men dead, and another man dying, the bandits mounted their horses and galloped out of town.

The brutal murders of three innocent bystanders enraged the entire county and an all-out campaign to track down the killers was launched.

During the course of the investigation, one member of a posse, a saloonkeeper named John Heath, sent the squad on so many wild goose chases the members began suspicioning Heath's motives. Under "questioning," Heath confessed he was the brains behind the robbery and identified his compatriots.[30]

The five who actually committed the crime were arrested, stood trial in the County Courthouse in Tombstone, and were convicted. They were to be held in that city's jail until their 28 March 1884 appointment with the hangman.

Because Heath did not actively participate in the robbery or murders, he was awarded twenty years' imprisonment, considered in those days a life sentence.

Cashman often visited prisoners, offering them solace and a compassionate ear for confessions or conversation whether the convicts were Catholic or not. The perpetrators of the "Bisbee Massacre" were no exception.[31]

As it happened, John Heath hardly had twenty days, much less twenty years, to ask the Lord's forgiveness for his sins, if that was his intention.

According to Anton Mazzanovich's memoirs, "The miners in Bisbee and Tombstone were not satisfied with John Heath's life sentence.[32] An organization was formed, called the 60-65 committee, who were to meet on a certain day in Tombstone. They were to storm the county jail and invite John Heath to a necktie party. The above was carried out to the letter, and Heath was lynched, [from a telegraph pole] after which the 60-65 committee disbanded."

The self-appointed executioners made no effort to disguise themselves. If any were worried about a resultant murder charge, Tombstone's coroner, Dr. George Goodfellow, put their minds at ease.

A hastily convened coroner's jury concurred with the respected practitioner's determination and ruled, "We the undersigned find that J. Heath came to his death from emphysema of the lungs — a disease common to high altitudes — which might have been caused by strangulation, self-inflicted or otherwise."[33]

The eye-for-an-eye dispatch of Heath did little to quell the populace's vengeful bent and anticipation of the multiple hanging. On the day before their scheduled demise, the men's confidences, to which Cashman listened, were punctuated by hammers thwacking and sawteeth gnashing through pine lumber.[34] A grandstand was being hastily constructed beside the gallows by local carpenter W. M. Constable. Five hundred non-transferable tickets, signed by Sheriff J. L. Ward, would entitle seated spectators to an unobstructed view of the convicts' execution.[35]

Cashman was disturbed by the sight of the plank structure and its image rankled her immensely. Frank Cullen Brophy's article, "Frontier Angel," acknowledged, "She knew the outlaws better than anyone in the community, and she knew how guilty they were. In the absence of a chaplain, she had actually baptized two of them while she helped the killers make their peace and prepare to meet their Maker. Nellie never worried about consequences. The only question she ever asked herself was, 'Is it right?' Then when she got the answer, come Hell or high water, she was usually ready, and went into action."[36]

Cashman knew a circus-like finale was not the only dread the five inmates shared. They had heard rumors that their bodies would be snatched for use as medical cadavers instead of staying in their Boot Hill resting place. She met with Tombstone's mayor and Sheriff Ward and convinced them a curfew should be imposed to prevent the hot-headed and, presumably, liquor-brave from inciting a riot.[37]

Then, after the Russ House closed for the evening, a gathering of miners listened as Cashman told them she believed the prisoners were guilty of the heinous crimes, but that justice would not be served by such un-Christian, inhumane treatment. Her deep and abiding faith probably caused her to also despair for the crowd's immortal souls if the grisly spectacle proceeded as planned.[38]

At about 2:00 A.M., Cashman and her recruits, carrying crowbars, sledgehammers, picks, axes, and doublejacks, slipped stealthily along the empty streets, advancing on the scaffold. Moonlight filtering from above the courthouse yard lent the structure an eerie, skeletal appearance. [39]

Less than an hour later, the grandstand had been reduced to kindling and tossed into an adjacent arroyo.

"Well, that's that," Nellie said approvingly. "There'll be no Roman holiday in Tombstone for *this* hanging anyway."[40]

According to Frank Cullen Brophy's reflective piece, God and Nellie, she said later, "When the mob showed up for the hanging, next morning, they found the bleachers and benches blown to smithereens. Nobody cashed in on that hanging, and when they called the show off, I think most of them were secretly glad we had stopped them."[41]

The convicted murderers were executed at the allotted hour and buried, but Cashman still feared their bodies would be exhumed and sold for experimental dissection.

For the next ten nights, under cover of darkness, two prospectors carrying bedrolls, a coffeepot, and a frying pan, strolled casually away from the Russ House.[42] Once out of sight, the pair veered toward the cemetery and camped there, protecting five fresh graves from molestation, keeping Nellie Cashman's promise to their occupants.[43]

FOUR

Tombstone's Busted Flush

If she did not already know it, foster mother Nellie Cashman quickly learned that parenthood offers an equal number of heartwarming and heart-stopping experiences.

Mike, the second eldest, was either the most high-spirited member of the brood or the most often caught at his escapades by his adoring Aunt Nell.

A vacant lot near the Russ House was the scene of one of his better-known schemes. The site was a gathering place for neighborhood boys to play baseball, but often as not, catcalls and score discrepancies resulted in punches and profanities, rather than baseballs being thrown.[1]

When the fracas grew loud enough for Cashman to hear, she hastened over, separated the pugilists, and commenced a lecture on self-control and sportsmanship. When assured that tempers had cooled sufficiently, she doled out slices of pie to seal the truce.

Before long, fake fights were being staged and the talking-to's suffered for the sake of a scrumptious sampling from the Russ House's dessert tray. The boys' reward was doubly sweet since they were undoubtedly convinced they were pulling a fast one on Aunt Nell.[2]

Another of Mike's misadventures could have ended less happily. He and a friend, both proud owners of their own burros, decided prospecting in the Dragoon Mountains was a capital idea. Visions of renegade Indians could not dispel those of finding enormously rich horn silver deposits, which filled the boys' minds as they packed and set off on their exploration without telling anyone where they were going.[3]

31

Although its name now heralds its original proprietress, like Tombstone, the Russ House's hey-day is long past.

Mike and his partner accomplished the fourteen mile trip without incident, and near sunset found an old cabin in the foothills to shelter them for the night.

With darkness came the glow of Apache signal fires dotting the mountainside. If a prowling scout saw or heard the burros, the boys might not leave the mountain alive, but thoughts of making their moonlit way back to town scared them witless.

After they had spent hours huddled in a far corner of the cabin, the sound of horses approaching must have seemed like a nightmare coming alive. Panic became pandemonium when Aunt Nell's "hello the house" sent them scrambling gratefully out the door and into her buggy.[4]

Miss Cashman's favorite nephew, Mike Cunningham, was one of the founders of the Bank of Bisbee (Ariz.) and cheerfully grubstaked many of his illustrious "Auntie's" prospecting adventures. (Photograph courtesy of the Arizona Historical Society.)

Fortunately, a prospector had seen the boys traipsing cross-country, recognized Mike, and reported their whereabouts to Cashman.

It should be noted that one of the larcenous pie eaters (and probably Mike's prospecting partner), George A. Mauk, became a U.S. marshal in Arizona. Mischievous Mike Cunningham's illustrious adult accomplishments included success in a variety of business endeavors, the Bank of Bisbee among them.[5]

While neither Cashman's good-hearted role modeling nor a crackdown on wretched excessiveness was responsible, by early 1884 Tombstone was losing its sinful luster.

Ironically, the one resource the town needed most, and had spent enormous sums to pipe from distant sources, effectively "busted" its booming mining industry: water.

The flooding of mine shafts exceeding five hundred-foot depths had been a chronic problem for years. Despite the installation of enormous and costly Cornish pumps to drain the tunnels, trickles became the veritable tributaries of a tapped subterranean lake or river. All the mines were affected and bailing was a futile exercise.[6]

As the alluvion worsened and mine operators' expenditures to divert it rose, the market price of silver was falling. Struggling for economic survival, the owners cut their miners' daily wages from four dollars to three.[7] Fearful and outraged, union employees of the Grand Central mine, one of the largest, retaliated by going on strike.[8]

Forever the miners' advocate, Cashman understood and sympathized with their grievances, but when she heard of a vengeful plot to lynch Grand Central's manager, E.B. Gage, her loyalties reversed. Convinced the situation had advanced beyond reasoning, she decided to scuttle the conspiracy by removing the intended murder victim from the scene of the crime.

With her pace and expression epitomizing innocence, she buggied to Gage's hilltop home on the outskirts of town and told him of the conspiracy and her proposed solution. The pair then drove through the center of Tombstone as leisurely as lovers on a Sunday afternoon ride.[9]

Once darkness cloaked the rig from curious watchers, Cashman hied the horses and raced pell-mell to Benson, where Gage boarded a train to Tucson and safety.

Again, Cashman saved a few hot-tempered Tombstonians from themselves while saving E.B. Gage from a premature demise. In so doing, she earned another heavenly sobriquet, "The Angel of Tombstone."

Yet not even she could circumvent a series of disasters befalling the town. On 10 May, the Safford Hudson Bank of Tucson failed and with it, its sister facility in Tombstone.[10]

The bankruptcies dealt a hammer blow to Tombstone, its striking miners in particular. Many were Safford Hudson depositors and the money they had saved, and now needed to live on, had vanished like a desert mirage.

As the strike dragged on, scores of miners quit the town to find work elsewhere. The decreasing customer base had a domino effect on Tombstone's businesses, including Cashman's.

With five foster children to raise, her income dwindling, and the city in turmoil, Cashman's Irish temperament must have been sparked when Constable Ben James served her with a writ of attachment 9 February 1885.[11]

John Smythe, a Russ House bartender, filed the lawsuit claiming his employer owed him $184.75 in back wages.[12]

A week later Cashman's attorney, Col. William Herring, filed a countersuit on her behalf denying the indebtedness and charging Smythe with breaching his employment agreement and defaulting on payment of money owed for room, board, bar and restaurant bills, and salary advances totaling $126.35.

Dating back to 1882, an itemized statement of Smythe's account included with court records shows the debit column mounting at times to several hundred dollars, but no entries affixing interest to the revolving deficit.[13]

Smythe's complaint belied Cashman's business philosophy as stated in an *Arizona Star* article: "She declared she liked men and found them always ready to play square with women who worked among them.[14]

"'But you can't take advantage of them,' she warned. 'Some women in business think they should be given special favors because of their sex. Well, all I can say after years of experience is that those special favors spell doom to a woman and her business. It gives me a feeling of pride to be able to go back to every place I've ever been and look folks square in the eye and know that I've paid my bills and played the game like a man.'"[15]

After a successful petition for a change of venue, the case was heard by C.E. Alvord, justice of the peace, on 17 February.[16]

Both parties named in the suit/countersuit testified. Then their attorneys introduced corroborating witnesses (the defendant's three to Smythe's one).[17]

With all evidence presented and counsels resting their respective cases, Alvord rendered his decision: "It is therefore ordered and adjudged that Nellie Cashman, defendant in the case, do have and recover judgment against John Smith [sic], plaintiff in the above entitled action in the sum of ninety two dollars and ninety-one hundredths dollars, besides costs and disbursements and statutory damages as follows to wit."[18]

The transcript offers no explanation why Alvord awarded Cashman $33.14 less than her countersuit demanded. Worse, Smythe's immediate filing of an appeal delayed payment until the court ruled on the action.

Records show Smythe's appeal languished for eighteen months until Cashman and he agreed to dismiss any further court action.[19] Partial victory though it was, at least the matter was settled and she was free to put Tombstone behind her — precisely what she planned to do.

Five months earlier, on the early morning of 12 May, the first of two screaming fire whistles sounded what was to be Tombstone's death knell. The sky dulled to gray as smoke billowed from the Grand Central Mine facility.

One witness said, "The draft from the shaft blew a column of flame and smoke high in the air. You could hear it roar."[20]

The inferno destroyed the facility's hoisting works, which raised and lowered men, equipment, and in some cases, ore from the shafts. More importantly, the heat turned its precious water pumps to lumps of scrap metal.

Within days, the whistle shrilled again when flames threatened the hoisting works at the Contention Mine, Arizona's most productive. When sparks fell into the shafts they ignited the timbers underground. Before the holocaust burned itself out, the Contention's pumps were also reduced to blackened ruins.[21]

With both companies' pumps rendered inoperable, water soon lapped at ceilings throughout the honeycombed tunnels. Because supply was already outstripping demand, silver prices were too low to justify the massive investments needed to refurbish and reequip the mines.[22]

The human stampede from Tombstone commenced at virtually the same rate its influx had, only six years earlier.

For all its hell-on-earth reputation, the town found crime flourishing more rampantly after the boom than during it. In a region where range cattle had always had a habit of "straying," livestock suddenly started disappearing from corrals and pastures. Shadowy streets and dark alleyways hid petty thieves, and anyone wandering beyond the city's limits was fair game for banditry.

When an insufficient tax base forced closure of the schools, Cashman locked the doors of her businesses for the last time. Foster children in tow, she traveled aimlessly northward.

A *Bisbee Daily Review* retrospective, with commentary from Mike Cunningham, described their meanderings: "At times they lived in mountain cabins in Montana and Wyoming where snow was piled nine feet high about the house. . .. Aunt Nellie was a prospector, herself, and did placering and 'worked like a Trojan' in her search for riches. Cunningham said she was rewarded with modest wealth, but she was constantly giving it away to the poor and needy and to various projects of her church."[23]

The gold fields Cashman prospected yielded the family's means of support, but as one early editor said, "Like a tin can, a mining camp often lies where it is thrown."[24] In most cases, restlessness, exaggerated hopes, false guesses, flood, and fire contributed to a settlement's quick demise before schools were either needed or constructed.

Edward J. Doheny "bootstrapped" himself upward from Cashman House dish-washer to one of the nation's wealthiest California oil speculators. (Photograph courtesy of the Arizona Historical Society.)

Rather than settling for a catch-as-catch-can education, Cashman chose to enroll the children in Catholic boarding schools in California.

Customers of the Cashman House in Kingston, New Mexico were treated to her cooking for a short while. There she met and employed Edward J. Doheny, and said of him later, "he was the best pearl diver I ever had."

That hardworking dishwasher went on to become a multi-millionaire oil man in California, but he never forgot Cashman and, in later years, grubstaked several of her Alaskan claims.

From Kingston, she migrated to the Harquahala, Mina Prietas and Preston fields in the Arizona Territory. Such geographic hopscotching was probably indicative of minimal mining success.[25]

More than a decade after the proposed expedition to Africa lost the coin flip to the Cassiar, Cashman sailed to that continent to try her luck at mineral mining.

In late November 1889, Tucsonians read this account in the *Arizona Star*: "Miss Nellie Cashman is visiting with Mrs. E.J. Smith of this city. Miss Cashman has just returned from a trip to Africa and is here in search of a group to accompany her to that country to explore a hitherto unheard of diamond region. Her reason for desiring help from Arizona is that men from this locality are more reliable, courteous and can endure more hardships than any men she met in her travels."[26]

Perhaps her complimentary recruitment prompted no takers, or Cashman may have exercised the female's prerogative and changed her mind. In any case, she never returned to Africa. Gold prospecting was her area of expertise and she did not deviate from it again.

Regardless of climate or terrain, the earth does not surrender its valuables without a struggle. Panning streams for gold is solitary, shoulder-stiffening, hard work. Even the most nimble-wristed prospector could swirl and rinse only a hundred pans in a grueling, ten-hour day.[27]

Good luck or bad, hands swell and burn from lengthy submersion in icy water. Eyes redden and tire from squinting to see specks of gold glistening in the pan's sandy residue. After hours crouched on a riverbank, knees and backbone crackle sharply and seem incapable of straightening.

Designs vary, but sluice mining basically incorporates a flume for diverting river water through a series of riffled boxes. Gravel is shoveled into the sections and the running water washes away the sediment, while the riffles snag the heavier gold flakes.

One or more prospectors can sluice simultaneously, but all concerned stand ankle- to thigh-deep in the unobstructed portion of the stream and heft tons of pebbled muck from its bed. At 1880s cost-of-living standards, if the riffles failed to catch an ounce of gold per miner, the day's expenses were not met.[28]

It is no wonder prospecting was often said to be "like hunting for a whisper in a big wind." The muscle-grinding labor and paltry payoff burst many a tenderfoot's get-rich-quick dreams. Experience taught hardiness and patience, but also inspired a dogged conviction that a plump nugget would surely glisten amid the next shovel's mire. Or the next. Or one of tomorrow's.

In many areas, an assayable amount of pay dirt had to be found before a claim (usually a fifty by one hundred-foot strip measured from midstream, landward) could be filed. Between loose-tongued officials and big-eared prospectors loitering in the assay office, keeping secret the location of gold-bearing diggings was nigh impossible.[29]

Cashman's diversifications prevented dependence on the land's elusive bounty. For prospectors accustomed to campfire-cooked beans and bedrolls spread on a rocky riverbank, her boarding-house's homecooked meals and tick-mattressed bunks presented luxurious and sought after respites.

Grubstaking her peers increased her odds of sharing in a rich claim, while prospecting herself whenever time and weather allowed, added an individual shot at prosperity.

In the fall of 1897, news of an enormous strike in the Klondike set Cashman's course for the next quarter century. Several weeks earlier, gold had been discovered in a trickling tributary called Rabbit Creek, near the wye where the Klondike River emptied into the mighty Yukon River.[30]

Prospectors fortunate enough to be in the area at the time came out lugging as much gold as they could carry and eagerly told their rags-to-riches stories.

On 15 September 1897, beneath the slug "Nellie Cashman Talks of The Klondyke," page one of the *Arizona Daily Citizen* carried this short article/entreaty: "'Going to Alaska! Well I [Cashman] should say I am. I was there two years ago and would have stayed only our provisions ran out, and we were in a portion of the country where it was impossible to procure provisions in less than three months; winter was coming on and I had to get out, leaving paying gravel at this place.'"[31]

The copy continued, "This is how she intends to go: She wants to stay there for two years, and will need five thousand dollars to make the trip and would like to hear from some body who is willing to organize a company and raise five thousand dollars for the enterprise. She will take six good prospectors and her mode of travelling will be heard from later."[32]

As it happened, two men later took credit for financing Cashman's Alaskan adventure. In 1948 a *Bisbee Daily Review* article claimed, "Aunt Nellie finally went to Alaska on a grubstake from her nephew."[33]

In 1924 an *Arizona Daily Star* story quoted an item from its archives, its interpretation arguably a left-handed compliment or pointed disparagement: "Nellie Cashman, the prospector, was staked by a Tucson man on her trip to Dawson. Nellie is a hustler. (Signed) Lew B. Hayes."[34]

From early 1898, anecdotes regarding her northern expedition appeared regularly in the Victoria, *British Colonist*.

On 15 February it reported, "The first white woman to penetrate the Cassiar country and who twenty-one years ago visited Alaska in quest of gold, arrived in the city last night from 'Frisco and is at present a guest at Burnes House. She is out now for a big stake, nothing more or less than the mother lode of the far-famed Klondike region.

"Miss Cashman is a lithe, active looking woman with jet black hair, and possesses all the vivacity and enthusiasm of a young girl."[35]

Later in the account, Cashman said, "My party is composed of my nephew and another young man, both robust, hardy fellows. However, I expect to be joined here by several others, and we will go North over the Stikine route in a few days. I consider it the best route to the northern country, and as I have travelled it twice when there were practically no trails, I know something about it.

"You would like to know how I dress when on such expeditions, eh? Well, in many respects as a man does, with long heavy trousers and rubber boots. Of course, when associating with strangers, I wear a long rubber coat. Skirts are out of the question up north as many women will find out before they reach the gold fields."[36]

Yuma's *Arizona Sentinel* paraphrased her plans as written in her letter to Mrs. Miles Archibald by saying, ". . . the intrepid Nellie said she would await the arrival of nephew Tom Cunningham. She expected to start for Skagway on his arrival, stickeen pass [sic] being mushy. She would go loaded light and would make the trip like a top; was feeling good and would write from Skagway. Many were returning disgusted and these Nellie styled 'tenderfeet.'"[37]

Three weeks later, a lengthy *Colonist* account, subheaded "A Bold Impersonator" showed that almost fifty birthdays had not dulled Cashman's wits: "Thomas B. Cunningham, of Seattle, came to Victoria last Monday expecting to be accepted as the nephew of Miss Nellie Cashman, the pioneer miner. It was a bold attempt at impersonation, but the would-be imposter did not count on the intelligence of his selected victim, and his plans were easily frustrated, but not until after he had secured a small amount of cash through his misrepresentations."[38]

Cashman corresponded regularly with eldest nephew Tom, but had not seen him for years. He was to accompany her on the trip to Alaska, but was late in arriving and his whereabouts were unknown. She heard he had been stranded in Seattle and wrote him there, but received no reply. A second letter to a merchant she knew there resulted in the wrong Thomas B. Cunningham being given her message and money for his transport to Victoria.

The recipient realized the mistake immediately, but thought passing himself off as Miss Nellie Cashman's nephew could prove profitable.

Cashman was wary the moment she saw the man declaring himself her sister's son. He said, in a faltering tone, "My name is Thomas B. Cunningham, and I have your letter," which he produced along with other identification.

She could not know the man's statement was technically truthful; his hesitation and nervousness piqued her suspicion.

"Your name is all right," Nellie said, "but you don't look like my nephew ought to."[39]

After a few moments, the petite prospector's intense scrutiny discomfited the man so completely, he confessed his taking advantage of the merchant's honest mistake and gave Cashman, according to the *Colonist*, "a pathetic recitation of his hard luck in Seattle, punctuating the story with sobs and moistening it with a few tears.

"The mining woman has a heart as tender as her nerve is strong and instead of becoming highly indignant and revengeful on the man who had defrauded and attempted to deceive her, she gave him her sympathy and proffered him some good advice. Cunningham had one dollar left out of the ten dollars which he had received and this he offered to return but was allowed to keep.

"'I could not think of sending him to jail,' said Miss Cashman to a *Colonist* reporter yesterday, 'though you may think he deserved it.'

"Miss Cashman and her company leave by the Centennial tonight for Wrangel, and will go into the gold fields by the Stikine route, that is if war between Spain and the United States is not declared before they get started inland.

"'In that case,' said Miss Cashman, 'I will return to the United States and every man of the company will return with me. I do not value all the gold in Klondike as much as I would a chance to fight those treacherous Spaniards.'

"'Would you want to go to war yourself,' asked the reporter.

"'I couldn't be kept out of it,' was the reply, 'and I would not only go myself but I would organize a company of women in the state of Nevada who would all go, and who would be of some effect in a battle.'

"Miss Cashman's enthusiasm over prospects of war became intense, and there was no doubt in the reporter's mind when he got through listening to some of the frontier experiences which she has already gone through, but that she meant every word she said."[40]

When the war ended (without Cashman's intervention) Colonel Steese, the U.S. engineer in charge of building roads in Alaska, had heard of her intentions to enlist.

"Why didn't you go?" Steese reportedly asked her.[41]

"I started to go," Cashman replied, "but your —— roads were so infernally bad that the war was over before I got there."

FIVE

"I'm Mighty Apt To Make A Million Or Two . . ."

In 1898 Nellie Cashman sailed to Skagway, an inlet seaport on the narrow neck of the Alaska Panhandle that had basked in relative anonymity until the discovery of gold in the Yukon. Naturalist John Muir likened the resultant rush to Skagway Bay to "a nest of ants taken into a strange country and stirred up by a stick."[1]

Dyea, 'the gateway to the goldfields' and a mere three miles distant, was next on her northward itinerary, but the Chilkoot Pass linking the two towns was rocky, ice- or mud-slickened, and practically perpendicular.

At an elevation of thirty-five hundred feet with overhanging, bottle-green glaciers and snowfalls of seventy-foot depths during the region's eight-month-long winters, the Chilkoot presented the ultimate test of human spirit and body, and inspired performance of some of the most extraordinary feats of the Klondike Stampede. The final four-and-one-half mile ascension was remembered by all who accomplished it for the rest of their lives.[2]

As if its treacherous topography were not enough of a challenge, the North-West Mounted Police would not permit anyone to enter the Yukon wilderness with less than a year's rations, about nine hundred pounds of supplies.[3]

Fifty pounds is a groaning load for most men to backpack up a thirty to thirty-five percent incline. Since the climb took at least six hours to accomplish, thirty or forty trips were needed to transport that nigh-ton of requisite provisions. Considering the frequency and severity of storms, a prospector could spend two months or more hiking his stores up the slippery shale divide.[4]

It is hardly surprising that the infamous Chilkoot defeated fully half the hundred thousand prospectors who challenged it — but it failed to foil a middle-aged, veteran miner named Nellie Cashman.

Unfortunately, by the time Cashman and others made their way through the mountains, winter forced encampment until the spring thaw.

As she explained, "We camped on Lake LaBarge [sic] till the ice went out of the Yukon [River]. We built boats and went down the Yukon to Dawson, going through the White Horse rapids, Five Finger rapids and all the others. Believe me, it's some journey, all right, to go through these rapids. I never want to travel any faster than I did there."[5]

In all, Cashman's wayfaring from Skagway to Dawson added another six hundred miles, by river, dogsled, and on foot, to an already extensive tally.

In his book *Klondike Fever*, Pierre Berton said the spring thaw and thousands of prospectors' arrivals turned Dawson, located approximately two hundred miles below the Arctic Circle, into "a city of sawdust and stumps and the skeletons of fast-rising buildings, its main street a river of mud through which horses, whipped on by clamoring men, floundered and kicked. In between these threshing beasts moved a sluggish stream of humanity. They trudged up to their calves in the slime, or they negotiated the duckboards that were thrown across the black morass, or they shambled in a steady flow along the high boardwalk that was mounted on one side of the street."[6]

Cashman wasted no time establishing herself in the gold-fevered frontier town: "I started a short order restaurant, which I called the Delmonico. All the old timers will remember it. Meals ran anywhere from two or three to five or six dollars. At that, I didn't make any fortune. Part of the reason, though, was because if a young fellow was broke and hungry I would give him a meal for nothing."[7]

It was Cashman's shareholdings in Number Nineteen, a claim staked below the incredibly rich Bonanza Creek diggings, which paid her handsomely.

"I took out over one hundred thousand dollars from that claim," she said, adding, "I spent every red cent of it buying other claims and prospecting the country. I went out with my dog team or on snow shoes all over that district looking for rich claims."[8]

Richard O'Connor's *High Jinks On The Klondike* related an amusing incident that occurred during one of those forays. According to O'Connor, it was nearing nightfall when Cashman arrived at a Stony Creek roadhouse. Following a hearty dinner of wild game and hot tea, she crawled onto a wall-anchored bunk sandwiched between a lower one containing a sleeping Indian woman, and an empty one on the uppermost tier.[9]

Sometime in the wee hours, a robust fellow heaved his girth onto the bunk above Cashman's. All was well until he rolled to one side.

Under such extreme duress, the canvas sling split end to end, sending the man tumbling down atop Cashman. Their combined weight then ripped her hammock, and the pair of them toppled onto the bottom bunk's snoring occupant. The native woman's ear-splitting response to the rude awakening was said to have sounded like "ten thousand devils," to which Cashman added, "I can still hear that squaw shrieking — it was the worst moment I ever knew in the Yukon."[10]

Although considered the country's only female mining expert, Cashman had no choice but to hire and/or partner with male prospectors on the filing or working of any claims she discovered. Mining regulations prohibited unmarried women from filing new claims; they could only purchase claims already filed.[11]

Yet for neither convenience nor companionship did Cashman ever marry, and a curious *Arizona Star* reporter once asked her why.

"Nellie's eyes twinkled as she replied, 'Why, child, I haven't had time for marriage. Men are a nuisance anyhow, now aren't they? They're just boys grown up. I've nursed them, embalmed them, fed and scolded them, acted as mother confessor and fought my own with them and you have to treat them just like boys.'"[12]

Always alert for income-producing opportunities, she bought out some "cheechackers" (cheechakos: newcomers) who had developed literal and figurative cold feet, and started a grocery store in the basement of Dawson's Hotel Donovan. [13]

"I found the uniform price of food $2 a pound," Cashman stated in an interview, that inflationary figure denoting the difficulties and distance involved in shipping goods to the Yukon Territory.[14]

One old-timer commented, "If a person were able to transport foodstuffs from Edmonton [Alberta] to the Yukon, he could make his fortune without ever leaving the comfort of his store."[15]

While her mercantile was definitely profit-motivated, the comfort of her customers concerned her more than a few extra pennies posted in the ledger.

To give prospectors an alternative to gambling, drinking, and carousing away the long winter months, she set aside a corner of her store, "The Prospector's Haven of Retreat," for reading and writing letters, and provided free cigars and tobacco.

Such generosity and thoughtfulness endeared her to the Klondikers and it was said Cashman's entrance to any establishment in town was a signal for every man in the room to stand.[16]

"I lived in Dawson seven years," she said. "That was a great place to meet interesting people. I met Joaquin Miller, Jack London, Jack Crawford, the poet scout; Robert W. Service, and lots of other well-known people up there."[17]

Now and then old friends from Tombstone, Wyatt Earp and Ed Schieffelin among them, came through town and visited her. In one case, a reacquaintance was accidental and John Clum included that reunion in his 1931 tribute to Cashman:

> Nothing was farther from my thoughts than that I would find among the women at Dawson anyone I had known before. The only inefficient article in my equipment on that trip was my camera. Darkness was imperative when changing the films. A genial photographer at

The "bum picture" as John Clum described it, of an older, stouter Miss Cashman posed in front of her Dawson, Alaska mercantile. (Photograph courtesy of the Arizona Historical Society.)

Dawson granted me the use of his darkroom for that purpose. While I was thus intently engaged a visitor entered the studio and addressed the photographer with great earnestness. Her appeal was for a subscription to aid the local Sisters' Hospital. I had not seen Nellie Cashman for fifteen years — not since we were both in Tombstone. But when the distinct tones of that rich Irish brogue reached my ears I recognized the speaker on the instant — and the nature of her appeal further established her identity. Forgetful of proprieties I called out, "Hello, Nellie Cashman! How did you get to Dawson?" Obviously Nellie recognized my voice as promptly as I did hers, for she called back to me, "Hello, Mayor Clum! Where in the world did you come from?" Since the days of 1881 Nellie had always addressed me as "Mayor."

The photograph I made of Nellie at Dawson with my inefficient camera showing her standing in front of her little store . . . is a bum picture, but anyone who knew Nellie will, at least, recognize her sturdy form. The features are not so good, but still recognizable — to those who remember.[18]

Another anecdote relating to her mercantile was published beneath the subtitle "Stars And Stripes Only Flag Known To Nellie Cashman, Even In Klondike," as a sidebar to a lengthier *Arizona Star* feature:

Miss Nellie Cashman related a little incident of her early gold rush days in Canada, while in Tucson, that was evidently a favorite with her, for as she finished, she thwacked her knee and laughed like a boy.

It was in the early days of Dawson, Klondike, when the mushroom city was celebrating an English holiday. Miss Cashman owned and managed a little grocery store and was busy when a burly, but faithful English miner entered.

"I say, Nellie, where's your flag?" he asked.

"Outside," she tartly replied.

"Beg pardon, but it's not. I didn't see a Union Jack as I came in."

Nellie, unceremoniously, grabbed him by the arm, marched him to the porch. She pointed to the Stars and Stripes hung from the wall, and several English postage stamps on which were the Union Jack, holding it up.

"There's my flag," she snapped, "and there's yours."[19]

As was the way of all boomtowns, Dawson's heyday eventually dwindled; for Cashman, this way a sure sign it was time to move on.

Fairbanks, Alaska, was her port of call for a few years, but as she recounted to a *Daily Colonist* [B.C.] reporter, "In 1907 I went to the Koyukuk district. I had a funny experience going down the river on a raft. I went down with an old sourdough. If you know anything about that river you know how many rocks there are in the channel and how swift the rapids are. In any event, coming down through some swift water we struck a submerged rock that wrecked our craft. It knocked all of the middle logs out. All we had left were the two cross pieces and the two outside logs. Sure, we got to shore all right, and fixed up the raft and went on. There is always something interesting happening."[20]

The Upper Middle Koyukuk River was known as the wildest, most remote area in all the Alaska Territory. Cashman settled there, some sixty miles north of the Arctic Circle, in a camp appropriately named Coldfoot.[21]

She never lacked confidence in her mining abilities or luck, and her every instinct told her Coldfoot embraced the mother lode for which she had searched so long.

"My boy, I've got it this time," she told John Clum's son-in-law, Peter A. Vachon, "and when I hit the pay streak in the shaft I'm sinking now, I'll strike it so damned rich that I won't know what to do with my money."[22]

Living alone amid Coldfoot's encompassing vastness would have been impossible for most people; as Cashman noted to reporter Bernice Consulich, "It takes real folks to live by themselves in the lands of the north. Of course there are some rascals everywhere, but up north there is a kindly feeling toward humans and a sense of fair play that one doesn't find here, where men cut each other's business to hack and call it 'competition.' It takes the solitude of frozen nights with the howl of dogs for company, the glistening fairness of days when nature reaches out and loves you . . . to bring out the soul of folks. Banging trolley cars, honking cars, clubs for catty women and false standards of living won't do it."[23]

At Coldfoot, and later Nolan's Creek, Cashman dedicated all her time and savings to finding her life's bonanza, but the shaft mining in which she was engaged required expensive machinery and the money to buy it. To attract investors, she formed the Midnight Sun Mining Company and sold shares of stock to help defray expenses.[24]

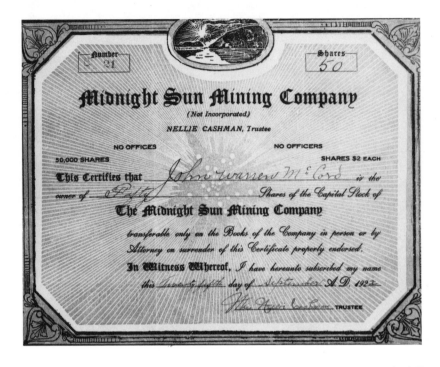

This Midnight Sun Mining Company certificate granted John Warren McCord a full fifty shares of Nellie Cashman's dream of an Arctic mother lode. (Photograph courtesy of the Arizona Historical Society.)

Every few years she left her top-of-the-world home to ferret out the capital needed to continue her mining operation. Among those always glad to see her and willing to provide a grubstake were old friend E.B. Gage and Alaska's so-called Bonanza kings, "Big Alex" McDonald and Jim McNamee.

Mike Cunningham also made certain his Aunt Nell never lacked for funds. According to Richard Woods, a Fairbanks banker, "On one or two occasions she gave me for safe keeping checks aggregating as much as ten thousand dollars. These were checks Mike had sent her, but because of her pronounced independent nature, she did not want to spend Mike's money — and, if I remember correctly, some of these checks from Mike were four or five years old."[25]

Regardless of who provided relief when her accounts edged toward red, the contributions were not couched as loans but more as indirect donations to charity. Cashman did suffer the "shorts" now and then because she gave most of her money to the less fortunate, sometimes at a faster pace than it was earned.

John Clum stated in his tribute, "they [Cashman's various underwriters] were quite sure that sooner or later, their gifts and her winnings [gold strikes] would all be disbursed to the needy and afflicted, to churches and hospitals, and, therefore, it was only a matter of time until Nellie would be broke again, and it would be up to them to provide her with another 'stake.' The fact that Nellie was never allowed to stay broke for any length of time is ample evidence of the high esteem in which she was held by those who so willingly aided her in those recurring periods of stress."[26]

Earlier in that account Clum included an "as told to" incident Mike Cunningham once shared of how one of Cashman's acts of kindness had benefitted him years later.

About the time the bank (of Bisbee) opened in 1900, an Irishman by the name of Con Delaney, outwardly a rather rough-looking person, came into the bank and wanted to sell his half-interest in the 'Broken Promise' mining claim in this district and asked me what I would give him for the interest. I offered him $500. In a very few, but very positive words he indicated that I might go to H——. He left the bank and I let the matter drop.

A week or so later Con came back to the bank and told me to make out the papers for the sale of his interest. I did so and he transferred his one-half interest to me for $500. I had the deed placed on record and this brought the transaction to the attention of Joe O'Connell, a local attorney. Joe called at the bank and asked me how much I had paid Con for his interest. I told him frankly — $500. Joe replied: "I offered him $750.' Of course, we were both curious to know why Con had turned down Joe's offer, so I looked Con up. I found that he was in poor health and actually

Miss Cashman in 1921 aboard the steamer Casca going down the Yukon River en route to the "States." (Photograph courtesy of the Arizona Historical Society.)

needed the money I had paid him. This made his action appear all the more mysterious until Con told Joe this story - which is true.

"In the early eighties I (Delaney) arrived in Tombstone from Ireland with my wife and seven children. We were destitute, and Nellie Cashman rustled up a place for us to live and provided food, etc. until I was able to obtain work. Nellie proved herself a real friend in our great need. I have never forgotten her kindness and this seemed to be an opportunity to get even with Nellie through Mike — so I had to turn down your (O'Connell's) offer of $750."[27]

Cashman's visits "outside" usually caused a flurry of newspaper coverage. After all, by best reckoning, her seventh decade was approaching, and at an age when joints creak and faculties fail, she still, "spread up her hard bunk in the morning, threw together soda biscuits, fried salt pork, boiled her black coffee and then worked furiously all day . . ." reported the *Arizona Star*.[28]

Earlier evidence of her wherewithal had appeared in the *Arizona Star*, datelined 24 October 1895: "Yesterday Tucson was visited, or rather revisited, by one of the most extraordinary women in America, Nellie Cashman, whose name and face have been familiar in every important mining camp or district on the coast for more than twenty years. She rode into town from Casa Grande on horseback, a jaunt that would have nearly prostrated the average man with fatigue. She showed no sign of weariness, but went about town in that calm businesslike manner that belongs particularly to her."[29]

Feature writers realized that human interest abounded in Cashman's tales of travel and travail, and often as not, the adventuress injected some of her matter-of-fact philosophy into the account: "I've suffered trials and hardships in the frozen plains of Alaska and on the deserts of Arizona. I've been alone all my life but I have been happy and healthy. That's why all are fooled by my age. And that is why I'm not afraid like most women to tell you that I'm sixty-seven and that I'm mighty apt to make a million or two before I leave this romantic business of mining."[30]

A 1919 newspaper article paraphrased Cashman's peppery observations of the changing world and "civilization" thus:

> After giving the East country the "once over" and taking two or three looks at the short skirts of the girls who had no tundra to mush over and the high heels they affected and on which no woman could ever accomplish the trail and arrive at the messhouse in time for meals, she had a dentist fix her teeth and came right away from there, back to the *everwas* land, which is so far away from California that California will never amount to much.
>
> Nellie Cashman knows that there are no hardships or privations in the world — that they are all in one's mind. She knows that things are never so bad that they could not be worse, and when she is thrown into association with people who have no pursuit but the avoidance or the treatment of influenza, and no pastime except the complaining or talking about the high prices of the straightform corset, it makes her peevish — she has seen and known life, and that baby stuff is not for her. She listened to their complaints of ill health, watched their eyes inflame and the tears run from them; saw them using innumerable pocket handkerchiefs to keep their noses clean, and then, disgustedly, advised them to get out of there and come to Alaska where life was life and not one nose wiping exhibition after another, and hit the trail for the North, leaving them to follow her advice and herself, or be miserable ever after.[31]

In 1921 Cashman was recommended to fill the post of deputy U.S. marshal. While she agreed she was better fitted to enforce the law than anybody else in the district, she good-naturedly qualified her reply by adding, "No, not the enforcement of the two-gun man. I wouldn't think of using force on anybody, particularly those boys up there. You see, they look on me as a sort of mother and they wouldn't think of doing anything wrong while I was around. I've been all through Alaska dozens of times but I've never been troubled by bad men. There isn't a man in Alaska who doesn't take off his hat whenever he meets me — and they always stop swearing when I come round, too. I wouldn't have any trouble in keeping order, because everybody's orderly when I'm around anyway!"[32]

A letter she wrote Mike Cunningham, assuring him of her safe arrival from a stateside visit, gives an inkling of her spirit, zest for life, and eternal optimism.

> I arrived here on the seventh of April (1923). I come [sic] over the mountains on a fast dog train and a native driver. The Northern Commercial company had every thing arranged for me. The sled only turned over once. I had a little roll in the snow. I dident [sic] see the party that I wanted in New York he was in Florida. I will see you late in the fall. I will remain here five months. I left my clothes in Fairbanks. I camed [sic] over the mountains very light . . . I am feeling fine after my long trip. It is snowing here today. We don't expect the breakup not before the middle of May (the spring breakup of ice on Nolan Creek). I am fixing up my cabin. I didn't move up from Wiseman (a town about one hundred ninety miles north of Fairbanks). I will go up in a weeks time then the cabin will be fixed and wood cut. My dear I've taken good care of myself. I got off the river before the breakup came and believe me I got off of it in a hurry. Mike drop me a line and let me know how yourself and the children are. I remain dear my dear Mike your Loving Auntie
>
> Nellie Cashman[33]

In January 1924, an Associated Press release trumpeted what would be her last trip to the United States: "Miss Nellie Cashman,

Despite decades of single-handed entrepreneurship and prospecting in gold fields renowned for their hellish heat or murderous cold, Miss Cashman looks more fiftyish than nearing seventy as she was when this picture was taken in 1924. (Photograph courtesy of the Arizona Historical Society.)

of slight figure and worn by years of prospecting and mining in the north, fully maintained her reputation of being the champion woman musher of the north in the opinion of pioneers here, when she came to Seward recently to take a steamship to the states. To reach Seward, Miss Cashman mushed, that is to say, part of the time she ran behind a dog sled and part of the time rode by standing on the runners, seven hundred fifty miles in seventeen days. In the seventeen days, with a good dog team and the lightning fast ice that precedes the heavy snows, she traveled along the Yukon and Tanana Rivers from Koyukuk, Alaska to Nenana whence she rode the cushions of the government's Alaska railroad."[34]

To lend a more modern perspective, the Iditerod's course is longer (eleven hundred miles) and the fastest time about six days shorter, but record-holder Susan Butcher had 150 highly trained Alaskan huskies at her disposal and was only thirty-six years old when she set the course's best time in 1990. Nellie Cashman had but one team, and was at least *seventy* at the time of her landmark journey from Coldfoot![35]

Later that year, when concluding her stay in New York City and Washington, D.C., Cashman traveled to Bisbee for a visit with her favorite nephew and his family.

When she arrived that city, she asked a taxi driver the price of the fare to Mike Cunningham's home. Told it was seventy-five cents, Cashman reportedly smiled, informed the hackie she'd walk, and started up the hill on foot. The driver was so embarrassed, he offered her a free ride to her destination.[36]

The warm southwestern sunshine must have soothed one who had spent over a quarter century in the frigid northern regions, but when family members pleaded with Cashman to stay in Bisbee permanently, she adamantly refused.

"I'm a long way from the cushion rocker stage," she remarked to one reporter, and on another occasion explained, "those prospectors up there need me — and need me badly — and that is the country in which I expect to live the rest of my days."[37]

As if to prove her dare devilry had not dimmed, she hitched a ride back to Nolan Creek on a mail plane. In his article, "Frontier

Angel," Frank Cullen Brophy said, "Not many ladies were making hazardous air flights in those days. Her relatives remonstrated with her. The old flame snapped in her eyes. 'What's wrong with that?' she announced rather than questioned. 'I was the first white woman there on foot. Why shouldn't I be the first white woman to go on an airplane?'"[38]

Cashman had said she caught a cold during every stateside excursion; this time, she could not shake its symptoms.

Exerpts from a letter written by Victoria's Sisters of St. Ann, chronicle her last months.

> Miss Cashman had been very ill of pneumonia for six weeks in the Hospital in Fairbanks, Alaska, before coming here; and it was only her great will-power which enabled her to rally and reach Victoria, as she said "to come to her friends, the Sisters of St. Ann, at St. Joseph's Hospital."
>
> She arrived here on October 9th, accompanied by Mrs. Adams, the wife of Captain Adams. Nellie refused to be taken to her room in a wheel chair, but walked in although she could scarcely do so. Nellie said she had been very sick and was "all in" and added, "I'm coming home to die." She was indeed a very sick woman, still we entertained hopes of her recovery. She suffered greatly during nine weeks but was always pleasant and ready to joke. . . . She never expressed the least desire to recover nor gave the slightest sign of weariness, no matter how much she suffered nor how tedious the hours may have seemed.
>
> . . . She had a weak spell, but Nellie rallied and was there for the two following mornings to say "Good morning" if not in words, by the light of her eyes with which she greeted her friends as they came in.[39]

Because Cashman had lived life to its fullest and was deeply devoted to her faith, she did not fear death. Instead, she happily anticipated rejoining departed loved ones and friends. "

If the eyes can mirror the soul, this final photograph of Miss Cashman reflects a wealth of good humor and gritty determination. Throughout her life, her credo remained as simple as her lifestyle: "When I saw something needed doing, I did it." (Photograph courtesy of the Arizona Historical Society.)

Sometimes I can hardly wait until I can get together Up There with all them fellers I used to know," she once said. "Say, won't we do some mining, though? And yarns? Why, I bet there's never been yarns like the ones we'll spin when I get there."[40]

If such an eternal reunion is possible, it commenced for Nellie Cashman on 4 January 1925. According to her wishes, Cashman was interred next to the sisters' plot, on a bluff overlooking the Pacific, in Victoria's Ross Bay Cemetery.[41]

Newspapers throughout North America eulogized her and a few bordered her obituary in black, a respectful honor usually reserved for public officials and high-ranking dignitaries.

The Victoria *Daily Colonist* said Cashman's "natural hardihood, a venturesome spirit, and a fearless disdain of physical discomfort fitted her for the rough live [sic] which she was to face, and . . . she stood the test magnificently."[42]

Declared the *Arizona Star:* ". . . she lived on through the years of hardships that would have broken many men, to the ripe age of nearly eighty, though reports given out were that she was seventy. Pioneers, however, count differently and declare their addition good.

"The 'old sourdough' has passed on, leaving many records behind — pioneer of Arizona, the first woman prospector in Alaska, the world's champion musher — but better by far than all of these is the fact that she lived — lived and enjoyed adventures that it is not given most the courage to taste."[43]

Nellie Cashman was inducted into the Arizona Women's Hall of Fame in 1984, but as John Gilchriese, former University of Arizona field historian, declared, "So many undeserving personalities are heralded today, while less flamboyant types who really contributed something to the history of our country go unsung. Her (Cashman's) indomitable spirit and compassionate heart led her to truly great deeds all through her life. She saved many lives and donated thousands of dollars to charity, yet she is almost forgotten today."[44]

Only a carved curbstone, inscribed *Nellie Cashman; January 4, 1925; 80 [sic] years; Born in Ireland,* marks her grave. It is not a proper epitaph for one who gave so much, expected so little, and lived according to her own advice, "never borrow trouble or draw interest on past mistakes."[45] Perhaps one day Alaska, Arizona, or British Columbia will erect a monument honoring the bonny Irish immigrant whose pioneering spirit, like her generosity and courage, seemed inexhaustible.

And perhaps Fred Dodge's eloquently simple regards will be chosen as an appropriate eulogy. As he said, Nellie Cashman was "a truly remarkable and admirable woman."[46]

ENDNOTES

PREFACE

[1] The tribute from which this quote was excerpted was sponsored by the Bank of Douglas, Arizona. No byline is credited within the boxed salute, but because Cashman's nephew, Michael Cunningham, was a founder of that financial institution, it is likely he contributed to its creation and possibly authored it.

[2] Harriet Rochlin, "The Amazing Adventures Of A Good Woman," *Journal Of The West* (April 1973) 282-83. Discrepancies concerning Cashman's appearance range from her height approaching Amazonian stature to blonde hair and blue eyes. Rochlin attributes these and other errors to reporters' tendencies to fill informational gaps with fallacies.

[3] Ivan Clyde Lake, "Irish Nellie, Angel Of The Cassiar," *Alaska Sportsman* (October 1963), 44.

[4] John P. Clum, "Nellie Cashman," *Arizona Historical Review* (October 1930), 33.

CHAPTER ONE

[1] Harriet, Rochlin, "The Amazing Adventures Of A Good Woman," *Journal of the West* (April 1973), 282-83.

[2] Thomas A. Brennan, Jr., *Born Under The Bell Jar: A Cashman Family of New York* (New York City Public Library holding, 1966), 2. Brennan multiplied the number of Cashman births in Ireland in 1890 (sixteen) by that year's life expectancy (44.7 years) to summate this estimate. By definition, the surname means either "one who seized people by the head," i.e., a sheriff's officer or bailiff, or a box or till in which money is held.

[3] National Archives microfilm, immigration lists of passengers arriving Boston, 1848-1891, M-265, roll 38, list 654.

[4] Ibid.

[5] Rochlin, "Good Woman," 283.

[6] Frank Cullen Brophy, "God And Nellie," *Alive* (October 1973), 2-3, 28. Brophy's father, W.H. Brophy knew Nellie well and spoke of her adventures and good deeds so often she seemed a member of the family. When *Alive*'s editor asked Frank Brophy to write an article about Nellie, he styled it as a letter from Nellie to God, rather than a typical biographical narrative, which allows a fascinating perspective on the elder Brophy's perceptions and rememberances of her.

[7] Ibid.

[8] Ivan Clyde Lake, "Irish Nellie, Angel of the Cassiar," *Alaska Sportsman* (October 1963), 42.

[9] Keith Wheeler, *The Railroaders, The Old West* (New York: Time-Life Books, 1973), 135, 138-41.

[10] Dee Brown, "The Transcontinental Railroad," *American Heritage* (February 1977), 17. Both the Union Pacific and the Central Pacific contracted their eating houses to private individuals, but set no standard of service. Gradually some stations earned reputations for house specialties, such as feather-light biscuits or fork-tender beefsteak, but many took full advantage of their famished, and captive, audience of customers.

[11] Ibid.

[12] Robert Lewis Stevenson, *The Amateur Emigrant* (Ashland: Lewis Osborne, 1977), 69.

[13] Oscar, Lewis, *San Francisco: Mission To Metropolis* (San Diego: Howell-North Books, 1980), 144.

[14] Dee Brown, *The Gentle Tamers* (Lincoln: University of Nebraska Press, 1958), 224. Brown relates that some men were highly critical of the privileges accorded women. Western juries would not convict a woman for any crime, even murder. "A white woman is treated everywhere on the Pacific slope, not as a man's equal and companion, but as a strange and costly creature, which by virtue of its rarity is freed from the restraints and penalties of ordinary law. In San Francisco there is a brisk demand for wives, a call beyond the market to supply. A glut of men is everywhere felt, and the domestic relation is everywhere disturbed."

[15] *Arizona Daily Star*, 7 January 1925.
[16] *Ely Record*, (Pioche, Nev.) 4 September 1872, 3:6.
[17] Rochlin, "Good Woman," 283.
[18] Brophy, "God And Nellie," 3.
[19] *Tombstone Epitaph*, November 1990.
[20] Ibid.
[21] Melanie J. Mayer, *Klondike Women: True Tales of the 1897-98 Gold Rush* (Columbus: Ohio University Press, 1989), 194.
[22] *Daily British Colonist*, 6 March 1875, 3.
[23] James Truslow Adams, *Album of American History*, Vol. 2 (New York: Scribner, 1966), 364. Nellie had no choice but to wear men's clothing. What the typical milady's layers of lace-trimmed drawers, chemise, corset, corset cover, bustle, flannel petticoat, four or five muslin petticoats, stockings, and a dress offered by way of warmth, was surmounted by impracticality and unwieldiness.
[24] *Daily Colonist*, 15 February 1898, 3:4.
[25] Ibid.
[26] Ibid.
[27] Ibid.
[28] Ibid.
[29] Mary W. Anderson,, "They Called Her The Angel," *National Tombstone Epitaph*, (November 1990), 11.
[30] Ibid.
[31] *Daily Colonist*, 11 January 1925, D-19. In response to a reporter's asking if she packed a sidearm for protection, Nellie said, "I have never carried a pistol or gun in all my life. I wouldn't know how to shoot one."
Interestingly, section B-2 of the 2 October 1975 *Arizona Daily Star* published an article entitled "Early Arizona Women: They Packed Pistols And Wrote Our History," and Nellie was one of the four gun-toting pioneers who were featured.
[32] M. Freligh, M.D., *Homeopathic Practice Of Medicine: Embracing The History, Diagnosis And Treatment of Diseases in General, Including Those Peculiar to Females and the Management of Children* (New York: Charles T. Hurlburt, 1884),

395-96. Symptoms of scurvy include debility, spongy gums, edema of the legs, foul ulcers, and livid spots on the skin; it is said to be caused by the "long continued use of salted meats and food of an innutritious and indigestible character, assisted by cold moisture, a pent-up confined state, want of proper exercise and pure air and such other means as tend to depress the nervous system generally."

[33] Brown, *The Gentle Tamers*, 195.

[34] Ivan Clyde Lake, "Irish Nellie: Angel Of The Cassiar," *Alaska Sportsman*, (October, 1963), 43.

[35] Richard O'Connor, *High Jinks On The Klondike*, (New York: Bobbs-Merrill Co., 1954), 89.

[36] Rochlin, "Good Woman," 84.

[37] Frances H. Backhouse, "Women of the Klondike," *The Beaver* (December 1988), 36.

[38] Rochlin, "Good Woman," 84.

[39] *Daily Colonist*, 11 January, 1925, D-19.

[40] Ibid.

——————— CHAPTER TWO ———————

[1] Editor's note, "Tombstone's Lady Legend," *Alive* (October 1973), 2. Ironically, a half century later Nellie "staked her last claim with the Lord" while a patient in this facility which her contributions and solicitations had helped to construct.

[2] *Arizona Star*, 11 January 1925.

[3] Ibid.

[4] John P. Clum, "Nellie Cashman," *Arizona Historical Review*, (October 1931), 10.

[5] Ivan Clyde Lake, "Irish Nellie: Angel Of The Cassiar," *Alaska Sportsman* (October 1963), 43.

[6] *Arizona Star*, 3 June 1880, 3:1. This friendly adios was followed two weeks later by an announcement that Nellie and a partner named Jennie Swift had opened a provision and fruit store in Tombstone.

[7] Walter Noble Burns, *Tombstone: The Iliad of the Southwest* (New York, Grosset & Dunlap, 1929), 5.

[8] Ibid., 20.

[9] Frank Waters, *The Earp Brothers Of Tombstone* (New York, Clarkson N. Potter, Inc., 1960), 88.

[10] Burns, *Tombstone*, 381. Called the Million Dollar stope, this tunnel was a Grand Central Mining Co. "glory-hole" which netted over $840,000. In 1908 the shaft caved in, carrying down an ice wagon and horse. Although the wagon smashed into splinters, the animal was uninjured and was led out through an underground passage to the old mouth of the mine a quarter-mile away.

[11] Odie B. Faulk, *Tombstone, Myth And Reality* (New York: Oxford University Press, 1972), 100.

[12] Waters, *Earp Brothers*, 89.

[13] Michael S. Durham, *The Smithsonian Guide To Historic America: The Desert States* (New York: Stewart, Tabori & Chang, 1990), 173. Clum made Nellie's acquaintance months earlier when he was the editor/owner of the *Tucson Daily Citizen*. Upon selling the *Citizen* and moving to Tombstone, Clum established the *Tombstone Epitaph* in competition with the eight-month-old *Daily Nugget*.

[14] Waters, *Earp Brothers*, 120. Despite his admiration for the Earp clan, Clum claimed his *Epitaph* was Tombstone's "law and order paper," and called the *Nugget* a "cowboy organ."

[15] Lonnie E. Underhill, *Tombstone, Arizona 1880 Business & Professional Directory*, (Tucson: Roan Horse Press, 1982), 4.

[16] Ibid., 5.

[17] Faulk, *Tombstone*, 97. Sixty-six stores, saloons, restaurants, and businesses were destroyed and the loss was estimated at $175,000.

[18] Ibid.

[19] Waters, *Earp Brothers*, 89-90.

[20] *Tucson Daily Citizen*, 5 April 1965.

[21] Carolyn Niethammer, "Frontier Restaurants, The West Wasn't Won On Beans Alone," *True West* (May 1984), 45-46. Whether the mosquito-speckled bowl Nellie ate en route to Arizona Territory was responsible or not, Niethammer points out that for all the Russ House menus advertised in the *Epitaph*, not one ever mentioned a bean dish of any kind.

[22] Burns, *Tombstone*, 33-32. Visitors and newcomers were surprised at the quality and variety of merchandise in the shops and stores. Where go-to-meetin' clothes were reserved for Sundays in most places, prosperous Tombstonians decked out in their best on a daily basis.

[23] Faulk, *Tombstone*, 108. Fancy transport was not required for the majority of the cemetery-bound, so Tombstone was never more than a one-hearse town.

[24] Carolyn Niethammer, "The Lure of Gold," in Western Writers of America, *The Women Who Made The West*, (Garden City: Doubleday, 1980), 74.

[25] Arizona Historical Society, John Pleasant Gray collection, manuscript 312. Mr. Gray thought it only fair to give credit where credit was due, and said, "the women of the camp's [Tombstone's] 'nether world' were the first to respond [to a call for help] and sometimes came near to bearing the whole load."

[26] Burns, *Tombstone*, 36. The Reverend Endicott Peabody, rector of the Tombstone Episcopal Church, once asked his flock for contributions to finance a fence around the churchyard. When gamblers at the Crystal Palace heard of the congregation's tight-fisted non-compliance, they donated a kitty comprised of chips deducted for all hands bettering two pair from the night's game. The estimable Mr. Peabody penned a polite note of appreciation for their generosity and the fence was erected, posthaste.

[27] Arizona Historical Society, John Pleasant Gray collection.

[28] *Tombstone Nugget*, 8 June 1881. In an Irish Land League meeting notice, Nellie is also listed as a member of the Committee of Arrangements.

[29] *Tombstone Nugget*, 30 October 1881.

[30] Ibid.

[31] Clum, "Nellie Cashman," 13.

[32] Ibid.

[33] *Arizona Star*, 11 January 1925.

[34] C.L. Sonnichsen, *Billy King's Tombstone* (Tucson: University of Arizona Press, 1972 ed.), 24.

[35] Burns, *Tombstone*, 37, offers another version of the incident whereby a disgruntled miner wields the weapon.

Donald Bentz's article, "Frontier Angel," *The West*, (July, 1972), 60, attributes the unsatisfied customer's role to Frank McLowry [*sic*] of O.K. Corral fame, but agrees Doc Holliday encouraged the diner to clean his plate.

[36] Frank Cullen Brophy, "God And Nellie," *Alive* (October 1973), 3.

[37] Niethammer, *Women Who Made The West*, 75.

CHAPTER THREE

[1] Oscar Lewis, *San Francisco: Mission To Metropolis* (San Diego: Howell-North Books, 1980), 112.

[2] Ibid., 139.

[3] A photo held by the Arizona Historical Society shows Cashman's home to be moderately sized (particularly for a family of seven), constructed of adobe, and featuring an adjacent gated courtyard, but notably lacking the architectural folderol so popular during this era.

[4] *Arizona Star*, 11 January 1925. Nellie referenced her busyness and shoot-out watching as having taken place during her short Tucson residency. However, a description of "wide open gambling places" and general rowdiness evinces a probable confusion with Tombstone.

[5] Odie B. Faulk, *Tombstone, Myth And Reality* (New York: Oxford University Press, 1972), 97. Faulk cites the *Epitaph's* (John Clum's) dramatic description of the devastation: "The blackened walls and smoking ruins of what were once handsome and beautiful buildings is all that remains of what was the very heart of Tombstone."

Townsfolk did learn their lesson. Within months, the Huachuca Water Company was organized by a group of Easterners to pipe water twenty-one miles from the Huachuca Mountains. The construction of an enormous reservoir almost four hundred feet higher than the town delivered a capacious supply at a pressure of one hundred sixty pounds per square inch, a wallop that could convert a smoldering miner's shack into matchsticks.

[6] Paula Mitchell Marks, *And Die In The West* (New York: William Morrow & Co., 1989), 57-58. Fire was the single worst threat in most boomtowns; a fact of which Nellie was quite aware. She was in, or near, Virginia City when two thousand buildings were destroyed and four people killed, and in Tombstone when the Arcade went up like tinder.

[7] Carolyn Niethammer, "The Lure of Gold," in Western Writers of America, *The Women Who Made The West*, (Garden City: Doubleday, 1980). 77.

[8] Frank Waters, *The Earp Brothers Of Tombstone* (New York: Clarkson N. Potter, Inc., 1960), 158-59.

[9] *Bisbee Daily Review*, 1 April 1948.

[10] C.L. Sonnichsen, *Billy King's Tombstone* (Tucson: University of Arizona Press, 1972 ed.) 17. Sonnichsen said the citizens of Tombstone were not ashamed of their town's reputation, just rankled by "having its sins taken too seriously."

[11] Walter Noble Burns, *Tombstone, Iliad of the Southwest* (New York: Grosset & Dunlap, 1929), 1. The author gives a poetic and chilling depiction of Indian ambushes: "Through desert mesquite and cactus, the invisible savages slipped with the noiseless swiftness of running water; like poisonous reptiles they wriggled upon their bellies to points of murderous vantage; as still as cougars and as patient, they lurked beside the trails or watched a cabin door."

[12] *Arizona Star*, 11 January 1925.

[13] *Daily Colonist*, 11 January 1925.

[14] Choral Pepper, "The Angel And The Golo Valley Gold," *Desert* (December 1975), 25.

[15] John P. Clum, "Nellie Cashman," *Arizona Historical Review* (October 1931), 23-24.

[16] Donald N. Bentz, "Frontier Angel," *The West* (July 1972), 60.

[17] Joan Swallow Reiter, *The Old West, The Women* (Alexandria: Time-Life Books, 1978), 170.

[18] Pepper, "The Angel And The Golo Valley Gold," 26.

[19] Ibid., 27.

[20] Frank Cullen Brophy, "Frontier Angel," *Arizona Sketch Book*, (Phoenix: Arizona-Messenger Printing Co., 1952), 178.

[21] Pepper, "The Angel And The Golo Valley Gold," 27.

[22] Ibid.

[23] Ibid.

[24] Clum, "Nellie Cashman," 24.

[25] Harriet Rochlin, "The Amazing Adventures Of A Good Woman," *Journal of the West* (April 1973), 290.

[26] *Phoenix Weekly Herald*, 14 June 1883, 2.

[27] Paula M. Marks, *And Die In The West*, (New York, William Morrow, 1989), 401.

[28] Faulk, *Tombstone*, 158.

[29] Ibid.

[30] Clum, "Nellie Cashman," 18.

[31] Ibid.

[32] Arizona Historical Society, Mazzanovich collection, folder 2, document 486.

[33] Sonnichsen, *Billy King's Tombstone*, 187-89. Dr. Goodfellow is portrayed as a "hell of a fine feller," a handsome, aristocratic gentleman as comfortable in the swanky Maison Doree restaurant as in a raucous gambling hall. Goodfellow published thirteen medical and scientific papers on subjects ranging from gunshot wounds in the abdomen and the impenetrability of silk to bullets, to Gila monsters. "He [Dr. Goodfellow] quite properly regarded himself as a foremost authority on gunshot wounds because of his daily and nightly opportunities for study and practice."

[34] Tom Barkdull, "Nellie Cashman," *Old West* (Summer 1980), 27.

[35] Faulk, *Tombstone*, 158-59.

[36] John P. Clum, "Nellie Cashman," 20.

[37] Mary W. Anderson, "They Called Her The Angel," *National Tombstone Epitaph* (November 1990), 12-13.

[38] Clum, "Nellie Cashman," 19-20.

[39] Brophy, "Frontier Angel," 178.

[40] Brophy, Frank Cullen, "God And Nellie," *Alive* (October 1973), 28.

[41] Ibid.

[42] Clum, "Nellie Cashman," 20.

[43] Ibid.

——————————— CHAPTER FOUR ———————————

[1] John P. Clum, "Nellie Cashman," *Arizona Historical Review* (October 1931), 20-21.

[2] Ibid.

[3] John Robert Murdock, *Arizona Characters In Silhouette* (Fray Marcos De Niza Edition, 1939), 88.

[4] Clum, "Nellie Cashman," 21.

[5] Ibid.

[6] Odie B. Faulk, *Tombstone: Myth And Reality* (New York: Oxford University Press, 1972), 165. A few years earlier, one "expert" considered it fortuitous that water was struck because it would relieve the mines of the expense of hauling ore so many miles to the river and would "bring more capital to Tombstone district than would a dozen 'big Strikes' in the upper levels of the mines themselves."

[7] Rufus Kay Wyllys, *Arizona, The History of a Frontier State* (Phoenix: Hobson & Herr, 1950), 289. A shrinking paycheck must have been doubly difficult to accept in a town where faro dealers were paid twenty-five dollars per six-hour shift, and overtime netted five dollars an hour.

[8] Paula Mitchell Marks, *And Die In The West* (New York: William Morrow, 1989), 401.

[9] Harriet Rochlin, "The Amazing Adventures Of A Good Woman," *Journal of the West* (April 1973), 289.

[10] Faulk, *Tombstone*, 168. Officials of the main bank in Tucson blamed the failure on the mining companies in Tombstone, while officers of the Tombstone facility blamed their Tucson counterpart's speculatory practices. The miners were less concerned with who was responsible than the fact that their money had vaporized. Tempers flared so riotously, a federal judge ordered a company of soldiers from Fort Huachuca to Tombstone.

[11] Writ of Attachment filed in Justice's Court of Cochise County, Territory of Arizona, 9 February 1885, signed by John Richardson, justice of the peace.

[12] Faulk, *Tombstone*, 70-71. With any boomtown's prosperity came a bumper crop of lawsuits. Tombstone was no exception.

More cases were filed during 1881-1882 than in years preceeding or following and most alleged claim-jumping, fraud, and nonpayment of debts.

[13] Smythe vs. Cashman: Statement of Account. This ledger sheet entered into evidence clearly itemized Mr. Smythe's debits and credits. At the bottom, a statement reads: "Mif [Miss] Cashman $126.35 which amount is claimed in her consideration is her answer as due over any amount due to Smith [sic]."

[14] *Arizona Star*, 11 January 1925.

[15] Ibid.

[16] Smythe vs. Cashman, transcript of docket in labor claim number 1061, filed 12 May 1885, in the district court of Cochise County, Territory of Arizona.

[17] Ibid. The record shows N.W. Fenton testified in Smythe's behalf. S. T. Anderson, Harry Miller, and A. Blois were sworn and cross-examined as Nellie's defense witnesses. Judge Alvord took the case under advisement until 17 February 1885 at 9:30 A.M.

[18] Ibid. Justice of the Peace C.E. Alvord's determination as transcribed in the court report.

[19] District Court, First Judicial District, Territory of Arizona, County of Cochise, 19 August 1886. Smythe's appeal is dismissed upon stipulation and agreement between the parties, each paying its own costs of the appeal.

[20] Faulk, *Tombstone*, 171.

[21] Ibid., 171-74. The owners of the Contention shut down their pumps after the Grand Central fire because they did not intend to shoulder the entire cost of draining the Tombstone mining district. As a result, the tunnels had been filling with water in the interim. With the loss of the Contention's equipment, the flooding became permanent for virtually the same reason. The cost of replacement pumps, approximately $350,000 each, was prohibitive, and due to the interconnective system of tunnels, whatever company drained its shafts would also pump the water from its competitors'.

[22] Ibid., 167. The Bland-Allison Act of February 1873 had artificially inflated the price of silver to approximately $1.29 per ounce. With the discoveries of vast ore deposits in the West, the price

began declining steadily, dipping below one dollar per ounce by the mid-1880s.

[23] *Bisbee Daily Review,* 1 April 1948.

[24] Stanley W. Payer, *Nevada Ghost Towns & Mining Camps* Berkeleya: Howell-North, 1970.

[25] Rochlin, Harriet, "Nellie Cashman, Gold Digger of '77," *Ms.,* (March 1973), 108.

[26] *Arizona Daily Star,* 23 November 1889, 3.

[27] Reader's Digest, *Story of the Great American West* (New York, Reader's Digest Association, Inc., 1977), 188.

[28] Ibid., 189.

[29] Ibid..

[30] David Reed, "The Yukon, River of the Midnight Sun," *Reader's Digest* (July 1984), 148. Rabbit Creek, appropriately renamed Bonanza, held one of the world's greatest concentrations of placer gold. By the turn of the century, more than fifty million dollars worth of glittery flakes, nuggets and dust, were harvested from Klondike creeks.

[31] *Arizona Daily Citizen,* 15 September 1897.

[32] Ibid.

[33] *Bisbee Daily Review,* 1 April 1948.

[34] *Arizona Daily Star,* 18 January 1924.

[35] *Daily Colonist,* 15 February 1898, 8: 2,3.

[36] Ibid.

[37] *Arizona Sentinel,* 16 April 1898, 1.

[38] *Daily Colonist,* 9 March 1898.

[39] Ibid.

[40] Ibid.

[41] C.L. Andrews, "Nellie Cashman," *Alaska Life* (April 1945), 53.

———————————— CHAPTER FIVE ————————————

[1] Pierre Berton, *The Klondike Fever* (New York: Alfred A. Knopf, 1958), 150.

[2] Robert Wallace, *The Old West; The Miners* (Alexandria: Time-Life Books, 1976), 211.

[3] Carolyn Niethammer, "The Lure of Gold," in Western Writers of America, *The Women Who Made The West* (New York: Doubleday, 1980), 82.

[4] Wallace, *The Miners*, 211.

[5] *Daily Colonist*, 11 January 1925.

[6] Berton, *The Klondike Fever*, 294-95.

[7] *The Daily Colonist*, 11 January 1925.

[8] Ibid.

[9] Richard O'Connor, *High Jinks On The Klondike* (New York: Bobbs-Merrill, 1954), 89-90.

[10] Ibid.

[11] Frances Backhouse, "Women of the Klondike," *The Beaver* (December 1988/January 1989), 36.

[12] *Arizona Star*, 11 January 1925.

[13] *Daily Colonist*, 11 January 1925.

[14] Ibid.

[15] James Blower, *Gold Rush 1894-1897, A Pictoral History* (Canada, LTD, McGraw-Hill, 1971), 93. An Italian fruit vendor's sanity was questioned when he laboriously lugged several tons of fruits and vegetables over the mountains to Dawson. His estimation rose appreciably when his oranges and lemons sold in Dawson for a dollar each.

[16] Donald N. Bentz, "Frontier Angel," *The West* (July 1972), 61.

[17] *Daily Colonist*, 11 January 1925.

[18] John P. Clum, "Nellie Cashman," *Arizona Historical Review* (October 1930), 28.

[19] *Arizona Star*, 11 January 1924.

[20] *Daily Colonist*, 11 January 1925.

[21] Clum, "Nellie Cashman," 33.

[22] Ibid., 32. Clum noted parenthetically, "that word 'damn' was the limit of Nellie's profanity."

[23] *Arizona Star*, 11 January 1924.

[24] Arizona Historical Society, Brophy collection, box 5, folder 143. A copy of a Midnight Sun Mining Company certificate number 21, dated 25 September 1922, shows John Warren McCord owned fifty, two-dollar shares of Nellie's dream.

[25] Clum, "Nellie Cashman," 33.

[26] Ibid., 34.

[27] Ibid., 35-36.

[28] *Arizona Star*, 11 January 1925

[29] *Arizona Star*, 24 October 1925.

[30] Harriet Rochlin, "The Amazing Adventures Of A Good Woman," *Journal of the West* (April 1973), 282.

[31] Melanie J. Mayer, *Klondike Women* (Columbus: Ohio University Press, 1989), 224, 226.

[32] Ibid., 226.

[33] Arizona Historical Society, Cashman collection.

[34] Mayer, *Klondike Women*, 226.

[35] *Bisbee Daily Review*, 1 April 1948.

[36] *Arizona Star*, 7 January 1925.

[37] Frank Cullen Brophy, "Frontier Angel," *Arizona Sketchbook* (Phoenix: Arizona-Messenger Printing Co., 1952), 180-81.

[38] Ibid.

[39] Arizona Historical Society, Brophy collection, box 5, folder 143, letter from the Sisters of Loyola, St. Joseph's Hospital, Victoria, B.C.

[40] Ivan Clyde Lake, "Irish Nellie, Angel Of The Cassiar," *Alaska Sportsman* (October 1963), 44.

[41] Harriet Rochlin, "The Amazing Adventures," 295.

[42] *Arizona Sentinel*, 8 January 1925.

[43] *Arizona Star*, 11 January 1925.

[44] *Arizona Citizen*, 19 April 1971.

[45] Ivan Clyde Lake, "Irish Nellie, 43.

[46] Clum, "Nellie Cashman," 33.

BIBLIOGRAPHY

Manuscript Collections

Tucson, Arizona. Arizona Historical Society.
  Brophy Collection
  Cashman Collection
  John Pleasant Gray Collection
  Mazzanovich Collection
  Manes Collection
  Museum Monograph: Woman's Hall of Fame, 1984
  Cochise County (Ariz.) Court Records, Writ of Attachment
    no. 1061, 9 February 1885.
Washington, D.C. National Archives
  Passenger Lists of Immigrants Arriving Boston Harbor, 1848-
    1891, M-265, roll 38, list 654.

Interviews

John D. Gilchriese, field historian, University of Arizona (retired),
  interview with author, 27 March 1992.

Newspapers

Arizona Sentinel (Yuma). 16 April 1898.
Bisbee Daily Review. 1 April 1948.
Daily British Colonist (Victoria, B.C.). 5 February 1875, 6 March
  1875, 17 July 1875, 16 June 1876.
Ely Record (Pioche, Nev.). 4 September 1872.
Phoenix Weekly Herald. 14 June 1983.
Arizona Daily Star. 3 June 1880, 23 November 1889, 15
  September 1897, 18 January 1924, 7 January 1925, 11 January
  1925, 2 October 1975, 21 October 1984.
Daily Colonist (Victoria, B.C.). 13 June 1883, 15 February 1898, 9
  March 1898, 8 January 1925, 6 January 1925, 11 January
  1925.

Tombstone Nugget. 30 October 1881.
Tucson Daily Citizen. 15 September 1897, 7 January 1925, 7 December 1929, 15 December 1929, 5 April 1965, 19 April 1971.

Articles

Anderson, Mary W. "They Called Her The Angel." *The National Tombstone Epitaph* 17, no. 11 (November 1990): 1-20.

Andrews, C.L. "Nellie Cashman." *Alaska* (April 1945): 51-53.

Backhouse, Frances H. "Women Of The Klondike." *The Beaver* 68, no. 6 (December 1988): 30-36.

Barkdull, Tom. "Nellie Cashman." *Old West* (Summer, 1980): 26-28.

Bentz, Donald N. "Frontier Angel." *The West* (July 1972):6-61.

Brophy, Frank Cullen. "God and Nellie." *Alive*. (October 1973): 2-3, 28.

Brown, Dee. "The Transcontinental Railroad." *American Heritage* 28 (February 1977): 15-25.

Clum, John P. "Nellie Cashman." *Arizona Historical Review*. 3 (October 1931): 9-35.

Editor's Letter. *Alive* (October 1973): 2.

Gilchriese, John D. "The Miner's Angel: Fabled Nellie Cashman: A Saint With A Temper." *Arizona Currents* (April 1966): 6-7.

Hazen-Hammond, Susan. "Nellie Cashman: Tombstone's Angel With A Dirty Face." *Arizona Highways* (February 1987): 36-37.

Lake, Ivan Clyde. "Irish Nellie: Angel Of The Cassiar." *Alaska Sportsman* 29, no. 10 (October 1963): 19-45.

McCool, Grace. "Nellie Cashman." *Gateway Times* (January 1962): 31.

Niethammer, Carolyn. "Frontier Restaurant, The West Wasn't Won on Beans Alone." *True West* (May 1984).

Peplow, Edward Jr. "Women Of The Old West." *Outdoor Arizona* (July 1973): 23-26, 43-46.

Pepper, Choral. "An Angel And The Golo Valley Gold." *Desert Magazine* (December 1975): 24-27.

Reed, David. "The Yukon: River Of The Midnight Sun." *Reader's Digest* (July 1984): 145-51.

Rochlin, Harriet. "Nellie Cashman: Gold Digger Of '77." *Ms. Magazine* (1973): 106-8.

"The Amazing Adventures Of A Good Woman." *Journal Of The West.* 12 (April 1973): 281-95.

Skow, John. "On, Hermit! On, Sluggo!" *Outside* 16 (March 1991): 58-64, 128-30.

Books

A Pictorial Souvenir And Historical Sketch of Tombstone, Arizona. Library of Congress Holdings.

Adams, James T., ed. *Album Of American History.* Vol. 2. New York: Charles Scribner & Sons, 1966.

Adams, Ramon F. *Western Words: A Dictionary Of The Range, Cow Camp and Trail.* Norman: University Of Oklahoma Press, 1944.

Berton, Pierre. *The Klondike Fever.* New York: Alfred A. Knopf, 1958.

Brennan, Thomas J. *Born Under The Bell Jar: A Cashman Family of New York.* New York Public Library Holding, 1966.

Blower, James. *Gold Rush 1897-97 A Pictoral History.* Toronto: McGraw-Hill Canada, Ltd., 1971.

Boyer, Mary G. *Arizona In Literature.* Ann Arbor: Gryphon Books, 1971.

Brophy, Frank Cullen. *Arizona Sketchbook.* Phoenix, Arizona-Messenger Printing Co., 1952.

Brown, Dee. *The Gentle Tamers.* Lincoln: University Of Nebraska Press, 1958.

Burns, Walter Noble. *Tombstone: An Iliad Of The Southwest.* New York: Grosset & Dunlap, 1929.

Dodge, Natt N., and H.S. Zim. *The Southwest: A Guide To The Wide Open Spaces.* New York: Golden Press, 1955.

Durham, Michael S. *The Smithsonian Guide to Historic America: The Desert States.* New York: Stewart, Taboni & Chang, 1990.

Faulk, Odie B. *Tombstone, Myth And Reality.* New York: Oxford University Press, 1972.

Fischer, Vardis, and Opal L. Holmes. *Gold Rushes and Mining Camps of the Early American West.* Idaho: Caxton Printers Ltd., 1968.

Freligh, M. M.D. *Homepathic Practice of Medicine: Embracing The History, Diagnosis and Treatment of Diseases in General, Including Those Peculiar to Females and the Management of Children.* New York: Charles T. Hurlburt, 1984.

Kane, Robert S. *Canada A to Z.* rev. ed. Garden City: Doubleday & Company, Inc., 1976.

Lewis, Oscar. *San Francisco: Mission To Metropolis.* 2d ed. San Diego: Howell-North Books, 1980.

Marks, Paula M. *And Die In The West.* New York: William Morrow and Company, Inc., 1989.

Mayer, Melanie J. *Klondike Women.* Columbus: Swallow Press/Ohio University Press, 1989.

Myers, John Myers. *The Last Chance: Tombstone's Early Years* New York: E.P. Dutton & Co., Inc., 1950.

Moon, William Least Heat. *Blue Highways: A Journey Into America.* New York: Fawcett Crest, 1982.

Murdock, John R. *Arizona Characters in Silhouette.* Fray Marcos De Niza Edition (Library of Congress), 1939.

Niethammer, Carolyn. "The Lure of Gold" in Western Writers of America, *The Women Who Made The West.* Garden City: Doubleday, 1980.

O'Conner, Richard. *High Jinks On The Klondike.* New York: Bobbs-Merrill Co., Inc., 1954.

Payer, Stanley W. *Nevada Ghost Towns & Mining Camps.* Berkeley, Calif: Howell-North Books, 1970.

Reader's Digest. *Story of the Great American West.* New York, Montreal: Reader's Digest Assoc., Inc., 1977.

Reiter, Joan S. *The Old West. The Women*: Vol. 23. Alexandria: Time-Life Books, 1978.

Sonnichsen C.L. *Billy King's Tombstone: The Private Life of an Arizona Boom Town.* Tucson: University of Arizona Press, 1972.

- *Tucson: The Life And Times Of An American City.* Norman: University of Oklahoma Press, 1982.

Stevenson, Robert Louis. *The Amateur Emigrant.* Ashland: Lewis Osborne, 1977.

Sunnyside High School History Club. *Arizonac: Petticoat Pageant.* Sunnyside, Ariz.: Sunnyside School District, 1971.

Thrapp, Dan L. *Encyclopedia of Frontier Biography* Vol. 1. Lincoln: University of Nebraska Press/Arthur H. Clark Co., 1988.

Traywick, Ben T. *Tombstone's Immortals.* Library of Congress Holdings, 1973.

Underhill, Lonnie E. *Tombstone, Arizona 1880 Business Directory.* Tucson: Roan Horse Press, 1982.

Wallace, Robert. *The Miners. The Old West.* Alexandria: Time-Life Books, 1976.

Waters, Frank. *The Earp Brothers of Tombstone.* New York: Clarkson N. Potter, Inc., 1960.

Way, W.J. *The Tombstone Story.* Library of Congress Holdings 1965.

Wheeler, Keith. *The Railroaders. The Old West.* New York: Time-Life Books, 1973.

Wyllys, Rufus K. *Arizona: The History of a Frontier State.* Phoenix: Hobson & Herr, 1950.